MIKE YARWOOD
IMPRESSIONS
OF MY LIFE

MIKE YARWOOD

IMPRESSIONS OF MY LIFE

with
Linda Dearsley

Fontana/Collins

First published in Great Britain by
Willow Books, William Collins Sons & Co. Ltd 1986
This edition first published
in 1987 by Fontana Paperbacks
8 Grafton Street, London W1X 3LA

Made and printed in Great Britain by
William Collins Sons & Co. Ltd, Glasgow

I dedicate this book to
Wilf Fielding

Acknowledgements
The publishers would like to thank the following people who have kindly loaned photographs for inclusion in this book: Sandra Yarwood, Josephine Brocklehurst, Thames Television (Tommy Steele, Frankie Howerd, HRH The Prince of Wales, Lionel Blair, Sir Richard Attenborough, Terry Wogan, Russell Harty, Dennis Healey, David Frost, Bob Geldof, Gorbachev, President Reagan, Mike Yarwood), front and back cover pictures.

Contents

1	First Impressions	1
2	Out into the World	23
3	Getting my Act Together	36
4	On my Way	51
5	Impossible Dreams come True	62
6	Pantomimes and Practical Jokes	78
7	Wedding Bells	90
8	'Look – Mike Yarwood'	103
9	Surviving the Seventies	112
10	Impressions of Royalty	126
11	Affairs of State	138
12	New Directions	149
13	Moving On	158
14	At the Crossroads	171

CHAPTER I

First Impressions

'Bunter!' roared Mr Quelch. 'Come here, boy!'

And Bunter, hands fluttering over his huge stomach, crept reluctantly forward on those curiously light, dainty feet.

'Oh Lord! Oh crikey, Sir. I didn't take the bananas, Sir, honestly I didn't.'

He was a stupid boy really because no one had mentioned bananas until then, but I and the other children round the TV set thought he was hilarious.

When the programme finished I used to run upstairs and put on the old school blazer that was too small for me. I would stuff a cushion up the front, wet my hair, part it in the middle and tease it into two Bunter curls on my forehead. Then I would pop a pair of wire-rimmed spectacles on my nose and I was away downstairs again in Bunter's mincing run, hands waving like stranded starfish.

'Oh Lord! Oh crikey, Sir! I didn't take the bananas, Sir, honestly I didn't.'

Billy Bunter was the Harold Wilson of my childhood. Of all the impressions I did to entertain my friends, Bunter was the one they demanded again and again, just as years later the audiences never seemed to tire of my impression of Harold Wilson.

It seems I've been doing impressions practically all my life. Apparently from a very early age I imitated my Irish uncles, the people in our street, the teachers at school and even the priest at our Catholic church.

On Sunday mornings when we got back from church I draped myself in my mother's embroidered tablecloth, put a cardboard mitre on my head and, clutching a brass bell and a few shiny items from our fireside set, I conducted 'mass' in the back garden. I strutted solemnly up and down, chanting in 'latin' and sprinkling the congregation with holy water from our fireside brush which I'd held under the tap just before the service.

My family and friends fell about laughing.

'Mrs Yarwood,' our neighbour Mrs Jenkins would say, 'he'll be on the stage one day. You'll see.'

And my mother laughed and shook her head. I was such a shy, nervous child that show business seemed the last career I would take up. I was so nervous I used literally to fill my pants when I was frightened about something, yet at the same time I could get up and do impressions without turning a hair. I don't ever recall being nervous about going on to the stage. I suppose I saw show business as an escape from my shyness.

I think it was the late Eric Morecambe who summed it up. Asked once for the secret of Morecambe and Wise's success, he replied that it was all based on fear. I know exactly what he meant. He meant a fear of failure. Just as soldiers in the war were more afraid of looking like cowards than of the dangers on the battlefield. The fear takes over and you either succeed or die.

I still get by on fear, the fear of being a total disaster, and that's what's brought me this far. I seem to have spent half my life with butterflies in my stomach.

I was born in 1941 in Bredbury, Cheshire. I was actually born at home, at 67 Broadway, and I've often wondered whether the people who live there now will ever put up a blue plaque like they did for Shakespeare!

My father was a fitter and he was away a great deal when I was young. He was never out of work but he had to go where the work was and so my older sister Josephine and I were brought up mainly by our mother.

Mum was a very attractive woman. She had golden blonde hair, very blue eyes and when she was young she used to be known as the most beautiful girl in Marple Bridge, a village not far from Bredbury. She'd come over from Ireland to find work and had taken a job as a nanny in a house at the top of the village.

She wasn't a trained nanny but she had a great many brothers and sisters and a special book on child care, the Dr Spock of the 1930s, which she stuck to rigidly. The children didn't seem to mind. Years later they wrote to my sister Josephine that Mum was the most beautiful woman they'd ever seen, and Dad was a favourite too because when he came to meet her he played tricks for them like hiding a lighted cigarette in his mouth.

My father also had quite a reputation. He was known as the local Romeo and when my parents first met my mother was warned off him by her friends because of his supposedly unreliable character. He must have persisted though because they were married in 1936.

They moved into a cottage in Marple Bridge. My sister Josephine was born and Mum continued to look stylish and chic despite the fact there wasn't much money. Josephine remembers the time Mum caused a sensation by being the first person in the area to wear the 'new look'. She walked through the door in 1946 wearing a long dress with a nipped-in waist, very high-heeled shoes and a hat. The assembled gathering was stunned.

Apparently I was an accident. Because of the war people weren't having babies, but somehow my mother found she was pregnant again and immediately decided we should move out to the country where it was safer.

Bredbury was in the heart of the countryside in those days and Broadway was a row of brand new houses. Number 67 was a red brick semi with a bay window, two small rooms downstairs and two small bedrooms and a bathroom upstairs. My mother, who had been brought up in old cottages, thought it was wonderful; so modern and new.

It was a very small house. I didn't realise at the time just how tiny it was. Now I wonder how we all fitted in. Josephine and I shared a bedroom and downstairs we all lived in the back room. The front room with its tiled fireplace and uncut moquette suit was for company and the Sabbath. The rest of the time we squeezed into the small back room along with the stove, sink, table and chairs, two easy chairs and eventually the TV set.

I don't remember much about the war years, although funnily enough when I first heard factory sirens much later on they sounded very familiar to me so I think the air raid warnings and the all clear must have registered on me subconsciously even though I was only a baby.

I was a quiet child generally, but at two I'm told I was already impersonating the woman across the road, a very large lady indeed, and members of our family.

I was also embarrassing my mother on bus rides. Apparently without warning I'd turn to an elderly passenger and say, 'Excuse me but can I try your hat on?' and as often as not I would ride all the way to Stockport with the old lady's hat on my white-blond head.

I think that must have been the start of my childhood mania

for hats. Every year at Christmas we went to the Belle Vue circus in Manchester and I was fascinated by the ringmaster's top hat. I used to love that hat, mostly I think because it shone. I would have loved to own one like that but ringmasters' hats are hard to come by and very expensive no doubt. Uniform hats with shiny bits on were almost as good and eventually a neighbour who worked on the railways gave me a hat with a shiny peak. I thought it was wonderful. I could spend hours just sitting there with this hat on. Then I would take it off, look at it, put it back on and start all over again.

One of my mother's favourite memories was of a time when I was four. I went off with Josephine to buy Mum a birthday present and came back clutching a tiny bag containing one bath cube.

'It was all I could get with four pennies,' I explained.

My own earliest memory is of my first day at school. Josephine and I were brought up as Catholics and I was sent to Josephine's convent school which took boys until the age of eight.

It was a fee-paying school and we weren't an affluent family but I think it appealed to my mother that I should be taught by nuns: perhaps she thought it might help me decide to become a priest. Not that she tried to push me into the priesthood in any way, but if I'd become a priest she would probably have been very pleased about it.

It was a very wet day and I remember a huge building and a long, long corridor and being taken to various classrooms. I ended up in Sister Hannah's class. She was a sweet nun with a kind face and I think I must have enjoyed my first day because I don't remember anything unpleasant about it.

It wasn't always so nice though, and later I discovered that not all the nuns were as sweet as Sister Hannah. Most of them were very strict and one in particular frightened us all. There was a big scare on one occasion when the Mother Superior died and it looked as if this nun might take her place. Everybody was dreading it then, quite unexpectedly and without warning, Sister Hannah was appointed Mother Superior instead. We were all overjoyed, even the parents.

The convent was actually in an old Jacobean house and it had a lovely old chapel complete with minstrel gallery and beautiful paintings, but you don't appreciate things like that when you're a child. All I knew was that once a week we had to stay behind for mass and I got very bored. It was bad enough having to go to confession on Saturdays and communion on Sundays, without staying behind after school as well.

The services seemed to drone on and on and one evening as we stood there, fidgeting and restless, I whispered to my friend David, 'I wish I was a Protestant. They don't go to church.' And one of the nuns heard me. It seemed it was the worst thing I could have said and I was severely punished.

I don't think nuns are as narrow-minded as that any more, but the reaction at the time reminds me of that joke where one nun says to the other nun:

'I wish I was a prostitute.'

'*What* did you say?' replies the other nun, horrified.

'I said I wish I was a prostitute.'

'Oh thank God for that. I thought you said you wished you were a Protestant ...'

But if the school services were dull there were also the highlights to make up for them. I was chosen to mime to *Albert and the Lion* in one school production, and in another I played the part of a postman delivering letters to the assembled school including the nuns who were sitting on the platform. I don't recall feeling nervous. My shyness seemed to disappear when I was being someone else and as a postman I could approach even the most feared nun with a confidence that would have amazed young Michael Yarwood.

I wasn't a good scholar. I lived in a dream world. I used to fantasise all the time, rather like Billy Liar, and consequently I couldn't concentrate on my work.

Once my mother was summoned to see Sister Louise, ostensibly to talk about my school lunches which cost five shillings a week.

'Now, Mrs Yarwood, you're wasting your money,' said Sister Louise. 'Your son is not eating his school meals. I suggest he brings sandwiches.'

And then she went on to raise the matter of my lack of concentration and the fact that I was always clowning around to make the other children laugh.

'And by the way,' she added, 'who is this Dick Barton we've heard so much about?'

The nuns obviously didn't listen to the radio. There wasn't any television then and radio was the big thing – in particular *Dick Barton Special Agent*. I never missed an episode if I could help it and the next day at school I ran through the whole thing, performing all the parts myself and even doing the background music.

I was never in any real trouble as a child, mainly because my mother was very, very strict; in fact, to be honest, Josephine and I were scared of her. We were too frightened to do anything wrong. That's not to say she didn't adore us, and she could be very loving and affectionate. She was also impulsive: once she went out for a loaf of bread and came back with a radiogram. She had a real Irish temper, and could quickly flare up. She was fanatical about discipline and determined that her children shouldn't show her up. She was also very particular about manners. She hated ill-mannered children and as a result I was the only boy in Bredbury who used to doff his cap to ladies and give up his seat on the bus.

I wasn't a saint of course, but if things went wrong it was usually by accident. Our next-door neighbour drove a grocery van and sometimes he used to take me with him on his delivery rounds. I enjoyed this very much, particularly as my father didn't drive and we didn't have a car – but then very few people in the Broadway had cars.

One Sunday after lunch Josephine and I went out into the garden and found that Uncle Harry had parked his van on the strip of grass between our two houses. Harry was working round the back somewhere, but the van was open and I promptly jumped into the driver's seat. I don't know what I thought I was doing, pretending to be a van driver I suppose. I grabbed the steering wheel and stretched my legs out towards the pedals, and then, just as I'd seen Harry do, I released the handbrake.

The next thing I knew the van was rolling forward down the slope and gathering speed with every second. Alarmed, I jumped out, and Josephine and I could only watch in horror as the van careered into the street, crossed it and crashed into the lamppost on the other side.

Harry was very good about it but my mother was angry, quite rightly really because someone could have been killed. Anyway although it was only two o'clock in the afternoon I was put to bed and not allowed up until the next day.

For some reason Harry Reeves was always known as Uncle Harry, but his wife was never anything but Auntie Reeves. Auntie Reeves was my godmother. A stout, formidable woman, she could also be very kind and she was always generous. Whenever you went to see her she'd always give you a piece of Cadbury's chocolate, a chocolate digestive or a taste of her shandy. Sometimes she'd give you half a crown as well.

We saw quite a bit of Auntie Reeves but the thought of making her cross was terrifying.

One afternoon I came home from school and my mother was out but she'd left a loaf of fresh Hovis on the table. I was hungry so, just like a kid, I tore a great corner off the loaf, all crusty and fresh, and ate it. When my mother came in and saw what I'd done she went mad. Apparently it wasn't her bread; she'd bought it for Auntie Reeves.

'Right, Michael,' she snapped, 'you will take that across to Auntie Reeves and you'll show her what you've done.'

I was terrified to do it and terrified to disobey and by the time I got to Auntie Reeves's house I was crying so much she could hardly understand a word I said.

'What's the matter, why are you crying, Michael?' she asked when I arrived red-eyed and snivelling on her doorstep.

'I – t-t-tore the corner off – the bread,' I managed to sob, holding up the mangled loaf.

Auntie Reeves was lovely about it. 'Oh, that doesn't matter,' she said and she took the loaf, tore the other corner off and handed it to me. 'Here, have the other side as well. It doesn't matter and tell your mother not to bloody well fuss.' (She did swear a bit did Auntie Reeves.)

I stood there chewing this lump of bread and crying and saying, 'I'm sorry Auntie Reeves,' all at the same time.

I wasn't an angel and there were times when I disobeyed my mother, but only when I was sure she wouldn't find out. Every year at Christmas for instance Josephine and I couldn't wait to discover what presents we'd got, and since Mum always hid them in the same place – her wardrobe – it wasn't too difficult to arrange a sneak preview. We waited till she went shopping then we raced upstairs to raid the wardrobe, taking care to leave everything exactly as we'd found it. Somehow it didn't seem to spoil the surprise on Christmas morning.

The other matter was food. I know my mother wouldn't mind me saying that she wasn't a good cook. She hated cooking, so much so that years later when she had the chance of adding a kitchen extension to the house in Broadway, she didn't bother. She wanted to spend as little time in the kitchen as possible, and couldn't see the point of enlarging it.

Immediately after the war of course there wasn't much

scope for even the keenest cook. It was mainly corned beef and sausages, but later when things got better we had joints of meat and roasts. To be fair my mother made marvellous roast potatoes and good, really thick gravy, but generally she couldn't be bothered with fiddly things. I don't recall her ever baking.

We always had fish on Fridays, and like all kids I hated cabbage and liver, particularly lambs' liver, which appeared fairly frequently. We weren't allowed to leave our food so I used to wait until my mother got up from the table and then I'd grab the liver and slip it to Shep, our border collie cross, who always hovered around at mealtimes. Shep swallowed it down like greased lightning. I never got caught and Shep never dropped it on the floor, so I could get rid of the liver, but the cabbage remained a problem. You can't give a dog cabbage.

When I was eight I had to leave the convent and with my friend David from across the road I was sent to St Joseph's in Stockport. It was an awful place. A slum school really. It was dirty and cold; all green-painted brick and stone floors and every teacher was equipped with a thick leather strap. I got the strap one afternoon for flicking mashed potato at another boy in the dining-hall. The strap wasn't too bad, I suppose; it stung for a while but it didn't maim you for life.

David and I were aristocrats compared with some of the other children. It wasn't their fault but they were very uncared for. A lot of these kids had had their heads shaved because of lice and their clothes were grubby and frayed. They were always asking for food or money.

'Give us a penny,' they'd plead. 'Lend us a penny.'

At playtime there was a supervisor who came and sat in the playground to keep an eye on the children. In the mornings she used to bring thick slices of bread and butter and hand them round. I couldn't understand it. I remember thinking, 'Really I don't need this,' but I suppose some of the children had gone to school without any breakfast and that bread and butter was their first meal of the day.

I don't think my mother can have had any idea what the school was like because she was usually very protective. She was more concerned that we should be happy and turn out to be nice people than with academic achievements. She certainly didn't encourage us to put up with unpleasant situations.

As soon as she discovered how awful St Joseph's was she took me away. She came to collect me one day to take me to the dentist's and one look at the run-down building, the filthy handbasins and my miserable face was enough to convince her. I never went back. Shortly afterwards I started at the local primary school.

Although I was a shy boy, I was never bullied. I wasn't the hooligan type but I tended to make friends with the hooligans because I'd rather have them on my side than against me. I clowned around and made them laugh but stayed out of the way when they went looking for trouble. To this day I find social situations much easier if I can bring some humour into the conversation. It's a marvellous thing to make people laugh. It doesn't matter whether you're getting paid or not – you still get a kick out of it.

I was fascinated by anything that resembled a stage. We had an old air raid shelter at the bottom of our garden and I used the inside as a dressing room and the corrugated iron top as a stage. I would round up my friends, sit them on the grass in front of the shelter then climb on top to give a performance. Even better was the garden of a friend who lived down the road, which boasted an old hen run. The chicken wire had fallen down but the hen house had a flat boarded roof which was still intact and looked more like a stage than the air raid shelter. When there wasn't an audience I was happy just to stand on those boards and pretend.

There was never any shortage of people to mimic: the priest, the teachers at school, friends and neighbours. Sometimes a neighbour would come into the house and I would get behind her and imitate her over her shoulder with my mother looking on. I was a mischievous little brat. Fortunately my mother is about the only person I've ever met who could keep a perfectly straight face while this was going on so I was never found out.

Best of all for new material were the movies. My father has always been very hard of hearing so he didn't like going to the cinema, but my mother used to take Josephine and me regularly. We used to go after school to the early evening house. I loved the Bob Hope Road pictures, anything with Fred Astaire in, and musicals – I saw *Seven Brides for Seven Brothers* ten times, I loved it so much. Afterwards, back at home, I'd fantasise that I was in the film and would replay it, acting all the characters. All kids do that to some extent – they come home and pretend to be whoever they've just seen, Hopalong Cassidy or Tarzan. I expect these days they're doing Rambo.

Unlike most children however I paid great attention to detail and I went to some lengths to get everything right. One of the first films I saw, at the age of seven, was called *Life With Father* starring William Powell, and to create Powell's dark, heavy moustache I scraped soot from the fireplace in the bedroom and painted it on my face. Unfortunately I didn't realise that soot was such messy stuff. By the time I'd finished it was all over the floor and all over me. My mother wasn't very pleased, to say the least. After that I made do with a finger held beneath the nose when I needed a moustache.

Despite the performances I was usually quiet around the house and most of my home demonstrations were requests.

'Michael, do so-and-so for Mrs Jenkins,' my mother would say when a neighbour came round, and at family gatherings she would encourage me to go through my repertoire. Every Boxing Day we gathered at the home of one or other of my aunties. The uncles would go off to the pub at lunchtime and again in the evening leaving the women on their own. They didn't mind, though – they were very close and liked being together, and since I was too young to go to the pub, I stayed with them. They used to make me perform for them and while I did my impressions they tried to make me laugh.

As I grew older I became football mad. I think it was my father who started it. He took me to watch Stockport County play one Saturday afternoon. I was only seven or eight at the time and a bit too young to appreciate football. When the band finished playing at half-time I thought it was time to go home and when Dad pointed out my mistake I didn't want to stay for the rest of the match. I'd had enough. Dad didn't get angry but it was a couple of years before he took me again.

I wasn't particularly close to my father as a child, possibly because he was away such a lot, but those days with him at Stockport County were probably the happiest times of my childhood. I've never known anyone as patient as my father. He was incredibly placid. He and my mother used to have rows but it was pretty one-sided. The only time I've ever seen him lose his temper was on a family holiday to Blackpool. We were watching one of the end-of-pier shows (Frank Randall I think it was) and apparently I was chatting all the way through it.

In the end someone behind us said, 'Would you mind keeping that kid quiet?' and Dad turned on him. I can't remember what was said but he more or less told this fellow where to go. I was proud of him. I thought, that's my dad sticking up for me. My dad's better than anyone else's dad!

It was odd really. My mother had him right where she wanted him but he wasn't afraid of another man.

People say I get my sense of humour from dad. I didn't appreciate his wit as a child because he had a very dry way of putting things which went right over children's heads, but now

13

he makes me laugh all the time. He's a very witty man with a droll way of speaking.

As a child of course I couldn't see it. The best thing about my dad as far as I was concerned was that he took me to football matches. They were the highlight of my week. I knew the names of all the players at Edgeley Park, the Stockport ground, and I got completely carried away with the game. It was so different in those days. There was never any trouble. If there had been a fight in the crowd it would have made the front page of the *Stockport Advertiser*.

Most exciting of all was the day Dad took me to see Stanley Matthews play for Blackpool. Matthews was my hero because by then I was a football fanatic. We went very, very early because he was the first football superstar and the ground would be crowded. We got on the wall at the back of the goal and Dad took me down to the corner flag because he thought Matthews would be coming down the right wing and I'd get the best view from there.

I couldn't keep still I was so excited. Up until then I'd only been to Stockport County matches, and they were in the third division north. It was pretty special to watch the big teams. We waited and waited, me growing more and more impatient as the minutes crawled by. Then at last the Blackpool side came on in their orange shirts and white shorts. Stanley Matthews, thin and fast, raced past so close I could have touched him. I leaned forward, eager to catch every move. Then, almost as suddenly as he'd appeared, my hero disappeared. After five short minutes he went off injured and we didn't see him again. I was bitterly disappointed.

But it didn't put me off football. With David from across the road, who is still my best friend although we don't see each other so much these days, I organised a football team, the Broadway Rovers. Our pitch was the field behind my house and everything was as authentic as possible. We didn't have goal posts, so old railings or a pile of coats had to do, but I borrowed a heavy roller and rolled the pitch, then I marked it out by scraping lines in the grass.

Professional football teams advertised their matches of course so I drew up posters, printed in my best writing: 'Broadway Rovers versus (whoever) …' and stuck them on telegraph poles and lampposts throughout Bredbury. Nobody came to watch us of course, but that didn't matter. The important thing was that real teams had posters and so did we.

Professional teams also transferred players and since I was the player/manager I was in charge of such transactions. I still feel guilty about the time I sold a player. A team from another estate wanted this particular boy but I wouldn't let him go without a transfer fee. In the end they agreed to pay me threepence. I bought myself some liquorice with it.

As well as being the player/manager, I was also the match commentator and somehow I managed to run up and down the pitch while keeping up a constant commentary in which young Yarwood featured heavily.

Yet despite all the preparation the Rovers' games were unpredictable affairs. Sometimes the farmer would come out and chase us off the field because it was supposed to be grazing land for his cattle, and the match had to be abandoned.

On other occasions young Yarwood got sent off. Usually footballers hit players on the other team but I tended to thump my own side, particularly the goalkeeper if he let in a goal, and since my mother (who hated such bad behaviour) could see the game from her kitchen window, I was often called in and sent to my room. The match had to go on without the player/manager.

But sometimes the matches ran their course and when this happened they ended with the ceremonial awarding of the trophy as all grown-up matches did. In this case the trophy was my dad's ashtray. It was a strange looking thing, shaped like a chalice, made of thick, silver-coloured metal and when you turned it upside down it had two grooves in the bottom in which to rest cigarettes. I don't know where it came from. Dad used to say it fell out of an aeroplane during the war. Whatever it was, cleaned up it looked like a trophy and it was often won by Broadway Rovers. When the Rovers failed to win, the victorious team didn't keep it for long – because the Rovers' manager insisted on taking it back to his dad at the end of the day.

Football played a large part during my childhood. On Sundays we were supposed to dress in our best clothes and stay clean, but sometimes if we weren't going to visit one of the aunties I was allowed to change into football gear after church and kick a ball around.

Stockport County matches were played on Christmas morning in those days too, which meant that on Christmas Eve I had to go to midnight mass so that I could miss the Christmas morning service in order to watch them kick off at eleven o'clock.

I wasn't so lucky at Easter. Stockport played at three o'clock on Good Friday, the time we were supposed to be in church for the Stations of the Cross, and my mother wouldn't hear of me missing it. I attended grudgingly, feeling very hard done by, but in fact, as my mother said, I wasn't exactly deprived of football the rest of the year.

As well as football, David and I were also very enthusiastic about cricket. We played in the road, bowling from one side to the other, and we used to play eleven-a-side games with just the two of us. It's amazing how you can improvise when you're a kid. An adult might ask how you could play cricket without a cricket team, but it was no problem for us. We had a scoreboard with the names of Len Hutton and the English team and the Australian team printed on it. We both wanted to be England of course, but we took it in turns. We had ten innings each. David would bowl and once he got me out, I'd walk in through the gate as if I was going back to the pavilion, write down the score and then come back out again as a different batsman. Once every member of my team had batted I'd take over the bowling and David's batsmen would come on. It was simple.

Birthday and Christmas presents were easy for David and me. Footballs and boots, bats and stumps and any kind of sports annual were always welcome.

I was growing up by now but I wasn't growing out of my shyness and attacks of nerves. Every Saturday Josephine and I took it in turns to go shopping. My mother wrote out a list and we went to the butcher's and the grocer's for the weekend food. I didn't mind the local shops where I knew everyone but if I had to go to a strange shop, I dreaded it. I don't know why but I was nervous about going in and terrified of speaking to the shop assistant. If I could possibly avoid entering a strange shop, I did so.

This shyness even interfered with my football. I joined a junior football league, the North Reddish Junior League in Stockport, and I played with boys who went on to become internationals. I wasn't a bad footballer myself although I was very skinny and got kicked about a bit. The league had a social club where you could play table tennis and snooker. The only trouble was I wanted to go to it but somehow I just couldn't walk through that door. I would catch the bus, walk from the bus stop and get right up to the door and then I'd stop. Inside I could hear the buzz of conversation. I could almost see all those people enjoying themselves and I felt sick. I just couldn't bring myself to open the door and walk in. Instead I turned around and caught the next bus home.

Once I even missed a match because the opposing team were strangers. I got as far as the ground where the match was to take place, saw all those people and I knew I wasn't going to be able to do it. I turned round and went home.

I think I must have inherited this tendency from my mother. My father told me years later that even as a young woman she sometimes had attacks of panic and was nervous about going into shops. Most of the time she was fine and the house was always full of friends and neighbours, but occasionally I came home to find my mother lying down in a darkened room with a migraine and an inexplicable anxiety.

In later years her illness became much more serious, but when I was a child the attacks didn't last long and I learned to creep around making cups of tea on her bad days.

Despite my interest in sport I still loved the theatre. My mother used to take us to the pantomime in Manchester and the Theatre Royal in Stockport, and on holidays in Blackpool we went to just about all the shows there were.

We had two sorts of holiday: caravan holidays in North Wales and boarding house holidays in Blackpool. I loved them both for different reasons. The Welsh holidays were outdoor affairs. We liked the novelty of the little caravan with two beds at each end and the mingled smell of calor gas and wood. The weather was usually fine and the holiday activities stretched late into the warm evenings. A particular treat was skating at the roller skating rink in Rhyl, but whatever we'd been doing, the grande finale at the end of the evening was fish and chips. I remember walking home along the front on those very hot summer evenings eating marvellous fish and chips out of newspaper and feeling the sunburn tightening on my back.

The Blackpool holidays were different again. We stayed in a boarding house overlooking the Central Station, a perfect situation as far as I was concerned because I could look out of my window and watch the steam trains coming in, smoke billowing behind them.

My mother was a great one for the shows and we went to

them all: Frank Randall, Joseph Lock, Al Read, Ken Dodd. I loved going to the theatre and most of all I loved that moment when the spotlights came on, the band started playing and the tension mounted because at any moment those scarlet curtains would part. Even then I was thinking perhaps one day when the curtains open it will be me standing there, and I was filled with a yearning for show business. Yet it was only a fantasy. I was well aware of that. I thought you had to be born in a trunk to go into show business. It didn't happen to ordinary people like us.

Television made a huge impact on me. In the early years very few people in our road had a set and those who did let their neighbours watch it. Josephine and I used to go to the Kenyons' for the children's programmes. We would knock on the door and ask, 'Can we come in and watch television please?' and they never turned us away. Half the children in Broadway would be piled in their back room silently watching the black and white pictures. There were never any squabbles over the choice of programme because there was only one channel – BBC.

It was 1955 by the time we got a set. It arrived at lunchtime and I rushed home from school to see it. It had joined all the other furniture crammed into our tiny back room and the first thing I saw when I turned it on was *The Cisco Kid*, an American programme about a Mexican bandit.

Television made a great impact on everyone. We all used to sit and watch it every night no matter what was on, and when visitors called the set stayed on regardless. Suddenly there were even more characters to mimic. Billy Bunter was a special favourite of course, but my subjects didn't have to be well known. Once a piece of old film from the 1900s was shown, in which suffragettes in long dresses raced round at twice the normal speed. I was fascinated by the hectic, jerky movements and I had to try them for myself. My mother was out so I

19

raided her cupboard for a long coat and an old fur stole and strutted round the house like a frantic suffragette.

We didn't completely give up the radio when television arrived. I still loved the comedy programmes like *Ray's A Laugh* and *Life with the Lyons* and Sunday lunch wasn't complete without *Family Favourites* and *The Billy Cotton Band Show*. After Billy Cotton died somebody once said that roast potatoes just didn't taste the same without him, and I find that so true, I always associate roast dinners with Billy Cotton and Jean Metcalf and I suppose I always will.

When I was eleven I failed the eleven-plus and was sent to Bredbury Secondary Modern school which happened to be right opposite the convent. David didn't come with me. He'd stuck it out at St Joseph's and gone on to another school.

I wasn't unhappy at secondary school. There was no corporal punishment but they didn't need it. When you left school you were given a testimonial about your character to take to your employer and sometimes if you really stepped out of line you forfeited your testimonial, which was serious. For lesser offences you got detention and a lot of lines to write out.

There were some real hard-cases at school, violent bullies who used to beat people up, but somehow I made friends with them and they left me alone. They nicknamed me Spiv because I'd taken to wearing a handkerchief sticking out of my top pocket, just like the businessmen on television in their smart city suits, but that's as far as the ribbing went. They were more likely to ask me to do an impression than to bully me.

I was soon established as the class jester. Whenever the teacher left the room for any reason I'd do an impression of him. The class would be in stitches by the time he returned but I was never caught in the act and I believed the staff were unaware of my games. I was wrong. I discovered the truth on the last day of school, when I was fifteen.

The headmaster and teachers assembled in the library and sent for me.

'All right, Yarwood,' said the headmaster, 'we know you've been doing impressions of us, so let's see what you do. Let's all share the joke.'

There was no escape and since I was leaving school and they couldn't give me detention or make me do one hundred lines, I went through my whole repertoire. They all laughed and laughed except the teacher I was doing at the time, a pattern that was to become familiar in later years. I'm sure most of my subjects think that I do other people well but I haven't got *them* quite right.

Towards the end of the last year at school we had interviews with the Youth Employment Officer to discuss our future careers. Show business was something I wouldn't have dreamed of mentioning. It would have been like saying I wanted to be an astronaut. It was a fantasy, fine for daydreaming about at bus-stops but not for discussing with employment officers. I had to come up with something sensible.

I wasn't any good at practical things. Dad used to say it would be no good me doing anything where I had to get my hands dirty because I'd be useless. My best subject was football but I was too young to join a professional team even if they'd have had me which was pretty unlikely. My next best subject was English so I decided I wanted to be a journalist. Every afternoon when I came back from a football match I wrote a report of the game for my own enjoyment. Then when I was fifteen I started sending letters to the local paper about Stockport County games and they printed a couple of them. I was thrilled. I thought, hey, something in the paper – I could do this, I could be a sports journalist.

It's ridiculous when I think about it now. There was me, couldn't go into a strange shop yet I thought I could be a journalist. I'd never have made it.

The Youth Employment Officer was of the same opinion but for different reasons. He said to be a journalist you needed O and A levels, which I didn't have. I told him I wouldn't have minded starting at the bottom and making tea, but he shook his head, and said it wasn't a good idea.

'You've got the gift of the gab, Yarwood,' he told me. 'You ought to go into selling. You should pursue a career as a salesman.'

I thought that was an awful idea. I thought salesmen were people who went from door to door selling brushes. My mother explained there was more to it than that. 'There are lots of different jobs in selling, Michael,' she said, but she didn't think we should stick too rigidly to the career officer's advice. The best thing to do was to see what was available.

In those days there were plenty of jobs around and with young people leaving school at fifteen it was quite common for parents to take their children to job interviews. My mother decided it would be good for me to experience city life so she took me into Manchester, bought a copy of the Manchester *Evening News* and ringed all the suitable vacancies. Then we spent the afternoon visiting the companies which had advertised.

At last we came to a mail order firm called J.D. Williams which was looking for a junior despatch clerk. I was interviewed by a Mr Marsden, a big man with steel tips on the heels of his shoes, which clicked when he walked. I don't know whether my gift of the gab was evident or whether my school character testimonial impressed him but I got the job. I was out into the world at last.

CHAPTER 2

Out into the World

It was pouring with rain the Monday I started work. I remember sitting on the Manchester train watching the water rolling down the windows and seeping in through the crack at the bottom. The old carriage was damp and cold and it squeaked loudly.

I felt sick. I'd been up very early to allow plenty of time to catch the eight-thirty from Bredbury to Manchester London Road (now Manchester Piccadilly), and I hadn't been able to eat a thing. It was my first train journey on my own, my first day at work and I was very, very nervous. 'This is it,' I kept telling myself. 'You're out into the big world now. You've got to get on with it.'

J.D. Williams' was a huge warehouse not far from the station and I walked slowly up to the entrance along with thousands of other people, all alarmingly grown-up. I couldn't believe that so many people could work in the same building.

At the main office I was given a card and shown how to clock in, then I was taken down to the enormous loading bay where I was to work. It was like being out of doors really because the loading bay was never closed, winter or summer. Parcels were brought in in big trucks and each parcel had a docket tucked into the string. My job was to remove the docket, enter the details on a sheet and load the parcels on to the British Rail van that came to collect them. The van would back up, the driver would sign for the parcels and off they'd go for delivery all over the country.

I earned £6.10s a week for that together with the use of the warehouse canteen which struck me as marvellous after school dinners. By the end of my first day I felt several inches taller and really proud of myself. I was one of the adults now.

I enjoyed working in the loading bay (except at Christmas when we nearly disappeared under floods of parcels), but I wasn't very good at my job. I made mistakes and eventually Charlie Marsden, or Mr Marsden as he was called to his face, moved me upstairs into the knitwear department. It was a cushier job really because it was indoors out of the cold and I had to address parcels and record the addresses and date of despatch.

They were all football fanatics in knitwear and the game was the sole topic of conversation which suited me very well except for one thing. They were all supporters of Manchester United or Manchester City, the big clubs, and I was continually sent up for being a fan of pathetic little Stockport County.

I didn't really mind because it was good-humoured ribbing, but all the same I couldn't help wishing that Stockport would do something spectacular to shut them up for once.

Then one great day in 1958 Stockport played in a cup match against Luton Town who were second in the first division, and we beat them 3-0! It was a red letter occasion, with headlines in all the papers, and my father and I who were at the match had sore throats on Monday from shouting so much with excitement.

I walked into knitwear on Monday morning hoarse but

24

feeling ten feet tall. They couldn't take the mickey now. Pathetic little Stockport County had turned into giant-killers.

I enjoyed knitwear even more than the loading bay. The work itself didn't interest me for long but the department was fun. I soon turned into the office jester. All along one wall in knitwear there were mattresses stacked up, and now and again people used to climb on them for 'a little kip'. It was known as having a 'skive', the first time I'd ever heard the word.

Skiving was quite safe because the knitwear den was hidden from view by floor-to-ceiling steel racks containing stock, and Charlie Marsden's steel-tipped shoes rang out a warning over the concrete floor long before he came in sight.

But this gave me an idea. I had steel tips on my shoes too, to make the heels last longer between repairs, and when my colleagues were skiving I'd creep away and come back through the maze of racks doing the Charlie Marsden walk. It fooled them every time. They used to leap off the mattresses, run back to their desks and when I appeared round the corner they practically threw the parcels at me.

'You so and so!' they'd yell (only they didn't usually say 'so and so').

Yes, I was quite happy in knitwear, but unfortunately Charlie Marsden wasn't happy with me. Apparently it got back to him that I was impersonating him and generally fooling around. What's more, my work had not improved. As ever, the trouble was my lack of concentration. My mind wandered, I was still day-dreaming and I made mistakes. I stuck the wrong addresses on the wrong parcels and customers kept complaining. In the end, Charlie Marsden sent for me.

'Well,' he said, not unpleasantly, 'we're not doing very well, are we? I think we'd better leave a week on Friday.'

I was devastated.

'You can look for a job in our time,' he went on. 'You can go out and take off any time you like.'

This was very generous because he could have made me leave at the end of the week and search for work in my own time. Looking back I can see that he sacked me in the nicest possible way but at the time I thought the end of the world had come. I felt deeply ashamed and also scared. How on earth would I tell my parents? My mother would go mad.

All the way home on the Bredbury train my stomach churned and by the time I reached the Broadway I knew I couldn't face doing it. I wouldn't tell them.

The next few days were very anxious ones for me. I left the house as usual as if I was going to spend another day in knitwear, but in fact as soon as I got to Manchester I was scouring the papers for job adverts and going to interviews. I think my mother must have suspected something because I couldn't eat. I was so worried that food just stuck in my throat. If I didn't get a job by a week on Friday I could see that I'd have to walk the streets.

Fortunately it was much easier to find work in the 1950s than it is today and after four days' searching I was taken on as a trainee rep by M. A. Jacobs' Wholesale Gowns and Mantles. M. A. Jacobs was a small family firm which sold clothes to the retail trade. The idea was that eventually I should travel the country showing our stock to retailers and winning orders, but since I kept failing my driving test I was permanently confined to head office where I showed the garments to customers in our showrooms instead.

The successful interview at M. A. Jacobs gave me the courage to raise the subject with my mother. I told her I thought the time had come for me to move on and that I'd found a job with better prospects. To my relief she accepted the news without question. In fact she said she thought I was doing the right thing, and that it was about time I moved up from being office junior. She didn't find out until years later that I'd been sacked.

However, the dismissal didn't teach me a lesson. Fooling around came so easily that it wasn't long before I was established as M.A. Jacobs' resident jester and soon I was adding impressions to my repertoire. I did imitations of the customers and they made my workmates laugh so much that I couldn't resist doing the boss as well. He had an unusual shambling walk; he shuffled along with his feet turned out like a penguin's, at such an angle that he often caught the edge of a wastepaper basket or a desk with his toe as he passed. He also had a slight Welsh accent and a cigarette welded permanently to the corner of his mouth. He was just crying out to be impersonated and I couldn't help myself. Inevitably it got back to him, but he was understanding.

The customers liked me because by now I was entertaining them as well, and although I wasn't a very good salesman, at least I helped to keep them in the showroom. I was allowed to stay and the boss himself used to get me to do impressions for the customers at times.

Yet for all that, I wasn't as happy at M.A. Jacobs as I'd been in my first job. Although my childhood shyness was disappearing I still found it a strain to meet new customers and persuade them to buy our garments, and the driving test was an added pressure. Every time I failed it reminded me that I still wasn't doing the job for which I'd been employed.

I wondered if there was anything else I could do and thought that football might be worth a try. I'd outgrown the Broadway Rovers by this time but I still played football with the local team, the Bredbury Amateurs. One afternoon I did an amazing thing, well, two amazing things really – I scored direct from a corner, twice. It was a very windy day, the wind was blowing into the goal we were attacking and I was taking corners and swingers on the left hand side. I was playing left wing.

Anyway, I took a corner and the ball shot straight into the

goal. It's practically unheard of in football and the wind direction had a lot to do with it, but my team was delighted. Then I took another corner and I did it again. Bredbury Amateurs won 2-0 and I was the hero of the match. I walked round Bredbury for the rest of the week, convinced that I was the talk of the town. Surely everyone must have heard about my two amazing corners and if they'd heard, well what else was there to talk about? It had to be the sole topic of conversation. I paraded the streets like a professional footballer, certain that people were watching me admiringly!

My triumph gave me the confidence to try my luck with the professional football clubs. I wrote off to Stockport County, Crewe Alexandra and Oldham Athletic. Stockport and Crewe weren't interested, but Oldham invited me along to their trials.

As usual I was determined to do the thing properly. I was already pretty fit because I was young and played football regularly, but I'd read that the pro's went into training before their matches, so I had to go into training too. The week before the trial I got going (it didn't occur to me that I might need more than a week). Every night when I got home from work I went running round the field at the back of the house – the old Broadway Rovers home ground of my childhood – and since I'd heard about something called weight training, I did a bit of that as well with two bricks. I had no idea what I was doing. It's amazing I didn't hurt myself.

I went to the trial straight from work, sitting on the top of the bus, daydreaming about the new life as a professional footballer that was surely in front of me. My only regret was that it was Oldham and not Stockport who'd invited me, but then when I was established perhaps I could transfer.

Nothing came of it of course, but I didn't do too badly. There were lots of kids there and nobody played a whole match. They pulled boys off and pushed them on and by the end of the afternoon they'd obviously got a good idea of our abilities. I was told to go away and put some weight on, because I was still a skinny kid, and come back when I was heavier. And in fact they must have thought I showed promise because they sent for me again when they held their next trials but I was away on holiday at the time and missed my chance.

I was clearly not going to be a professional footballer, so it was back to the driving lessons, and another effort to concentrate on being a salesman. But my disappointment wasn't too great because around this time I discovered another interest – girls. Until then I'd been too wrapped up in football and cricket and too shy to do more than fancy girls from afar. Everything changed when I met Kevin.

Kevin lived on our estate but he'd gone to grammar school and we saw very little of each other until the day we met on the Manchester train. Kevin had a good education and a good job as a trainee accountant but he didn't bitch about it or make me feel small. He was a good friend and, better still, he was very popular with the girls.

He had black wavy hair that he wore slicked back with Brylcream like his idol Elvis Presley, and he was very good at chatting up girls. I was never an Elvis Presley fan myself, but I wore my hair slicked back with Tru-Gel which smelled nicer than Brylcream in my opinion and I tagged along with Kevin because I hadn't a clue about chatting up and I'd never have done it on my own.

Saturday was the big night. Saturday morning you had your weekly bath – the rest of the week you smothered Tru-Gel or Brylcream on your hair and felt clean because you smelled good. Then in the evening you put on your best clothes. Kevin usually wore a double-breasted blazer and an old school tie and I wore something similar until I got my three button Italian suit – a dark blue outfit from Burtons with a jacket shaped like a box. My mother hated it! Then we'd meet at the bus-stop for the red 33 into Manchester. We sat on the top deck smoking

Senior Service in ten-packs and joking about the prospects of conquests during the night ahead.

Usually we went to the Elizabethan Ballroom in Belle Vue. It was an enormous great room with a big staircase leading down and twirling glitter balls on the ceiling. Looking back it was just like a cattle market. The girls sat round the edge and the fellas walked around looking at them or stood drinking at the bar where you could sink as many as two pints in an evening and risk a real hangover the next day.

In those days the girls dressed very much like their mothers. A bit later there were beehive hair dos and big wide skirts but in the Manchester of 1957 fashion for girls wasn't striking. It didn't matter. At that age there was only one thing you looked for and that was a big chest. The bigger the better. The rest of the girl could be pretty grotty really but if she had a big chest it was fantastic. The idea was that you took her to the cinema and sat with your arm round her shoulders, gradually sneaking your hand down and down towards her chest ...

But first, of course, you had to do the chatting up. I used to think how great it would be if it wasn't protocol for the fellas to ask the girls to dance, but the other way round instead. It would make life so much easier. All that walking past and not doing it and walking back and missing it again. All that 'Right, I'll go this time and I'll *definitely* ask would she like to dance' – and still not managing to get the words out.

Kevin didn't seem to find it so difficult.

'Kevin, why don't you chat to those two?' I used to suggest after a couple of circuits, and as often as not Kevin would oblige.

After a while we made up a regular foursome. Kevin found himself a girlfriend called Gloria and I went out with her friend Barbara. Barbara was very nice but it was Gloria I really liked. She had fair, curly hair and a fondness for garments with fur collars. Matching skirts and tops, and fur collars. I thought she was terrific.

Eventually when Kevin and Gloria split up I was able to move in. I forget how I managed it now. I probably got Kevin to arrange it for me but soon Gloria was my girlfriend and I treated her to nights at the cinema, the Kardomah coffee bar or the Elizabethan Ballroom. You didn't take a girl out for a meal. You couldn't afford it.

In fact I found it difficult to afford even these modest evenings out. I was always broke and eventually I realised there was only one solution. I'd have to get a Saturday job. This was a drastic decision because it meant giving up my afternoons watching Stockport County, but I needed the money.

I became a Saturday assistant at the Stone Dry Direct Raincoat Company in Market Street, Manchester for thirty shillings a day, and soon afterwards Stockport County started playing on a Friday night which was great because it meant that I could watch them *and* earn the extra money as well.

The highlight of Saturdays at the Stone Dry Direct Raincoat Company was working with Tommy Dunbar. Tommy was a real character with a marvellously silly sense of humour. A neat, dapper man with jet black hair, white collar and a little black tashe, he always addressed me as Mr Yarwood and I always addressed him as Mr Dunbar. It was always Mr Yarwood and Mr Dunbar, even in the pub after work. The only time it varied was when we went into our rehearsed double act, invented by Tommy, in which we called ourselves Mr Hacky and Mr Tacky.

'Is this raincoat washable?' the customer would ask, because most of them were a pale creamy colour that would soon show the dirt.

'Oh yes,' I would say, 'they're washable. You wash yours, don't you, Mr Tacky?'

'Oh yes, I wash mine in the bath you know, Mr Hacky,' Tommy Dunbar would reply, as he solemnly brushed coats on the rails. 'Mind you, I have to take the coal out first.'

Tommy Dunbar taught me lots of little tricks. Sometimes a customer put on a size 38 coat and, finding it a little tight, asked to try the next size up, a 40. This was fine if we had a 40 but if we didn't Tommy simply brought him another 38 which usually turned out to be just the right size.

'It fits you like a glove,' Mr Tacky would say.

'Yes, a boxing glove,' Mr Hacky would invariably chip in.

At other times customers asked me to try on the coats so they could see them from a different perspective.

'Ah, doesn't he look well in good clothes,' Mr Tacky would sigh as I paraded up and down.

It was imperative to keep a straight face during these exchanges and we usually managed it, although we often cracked up when the shop door closed. I loved it. The frustrated performer in me couldn't wait to slip into the character of Mr Hacky.

After work we went to the pub together where even the most ordinary conversations sounded funny when they were conducted in Mr Dunbar's formal style.

'What will you have to drink, Mr Dunbar?'

'A pint would be very nice thank you, Mr Yarwood.'

Later we walked back to the station together where I bought a current affairs magazine large enough to conceal a copy of *Parade*, an innocuous (by today's standards) girlie magazine filled with black and white pictures of topless girls. I travelled home to Bredbury, apparently deep in serious reading, but in fact dazzled by all those big chests. If I'd seen Samantha Fox when I was eighteen I'm sure I'd have been head over heels in love with her.

Yet despite all the distractions I never lost my interest in show business. I would have been happy to do anything if I could be a performer but I had no idea where to begin. Music however was a different matter. Elvis Presley in America and people like Cliff Richard and Adam Faith in Britain had proved that ordinary people could do well as performers in the music business and they'd shown how it was done. You started a pop group, played at dances and got discovered.

I wasn't particularly musical myself but the idea of a pop career had certainly crossed my mind and a lot of other lads were obviously thinking along the same lines.

One morning I bumped into Brian Healy, an old school friend, on the morning train. We all seemed to work in Manchester so these reunions were quite common. This particular morning Brian and I got talking and discovered that we'd both been thinking about starting a pop group. Brian said that his friend Mike Medina who also worked in Manchester would be interested too and by the end of the journey the Drum Beats had been formed.

Brian had a guitar, Mike played the piano and I bought a second-hand snare drum which was badly out of tune, as well as a set of brushes, some sticks and a high hat. I couldn't actually play the drums so I thought I'd have a few lessons. I'd pick it up in no time I was sure.

I was in for a shock. When I went along for my first lesson I was told you have to be able to read music. I couldn't believe it. How can you possibly write music for drums, I wondered. It turned out that you could and they did and since I couldn't read music it seemed pointless to carry on. I abandoned the lessons and decided to teach myself at home.

I moved my drumkit into the front room and sat for hours playing along with records on the radiogram and annoying the neighbours. My mother wasn't too bad about it although she couldn't have enjoyed my music. Probably she thought that anything that kept me off the streets was healthy. The sticks proved too difficult to master so I tended to keep to the brushes which were easier, and I was quite pleased with my progress. If I turned the radiogram up really loud it sounded pretty good.

Soon the Drum Beats were practising regularly at Brian's house in his front room. We must have made a hell of a noise but his mother was very patient and we thought we were wonderful. We really thought something exciting might happen. I expect the Beatles started the same way. The only difference was that the Beatles were good and we were terrible!

Undeterred we started going for auditions in pubs and working-men's clubs all over Bredbury and Manchester. It wasn't easy lugging our equipment on and off buses while the conductor tapped his foot impatiently and the snare drum got stuck in the stairwell, but we were sure that it was only a matter of time before we were discovered.

Brian was a Lonnie Donegan fan at the time so we did a lot of skiffle numbers, but just to show how versatile we were I sometimes came off the drums and did singing impersonations of Cliff Richard and Adam Faith (I'm still amazed to think that as a kid I was impersonating top pop stars who're still around today).

We didn't have any success at all. In fact we were a disaster. I don't think we got a single booking. We only ever did auditions and some of them were so bad we weren't allowed to finish. At one working-man's club we'd planned to run through three numbers to give them the full flavour of our act, but after the first song the concert chairman stood up and snatched the microphone.

'That's enough of that rubbish,' he said firmly and we were left to remove our instruments and make our way back to the bus-stop. We didn't get the booking.

Looking back, it's incredible how long we persisted in the face of such complete lack of encouragement, but eventually even the optimism of the Drum Beats couldn't blind us to the truth. We were never going to do well in the music business and we were wasting our time. After this realisation the group gradually fizzled out.

My pop career, like my football career, was clearly a non-starter, and I'd have to find another way of becoming a star. It was back to the drawing board.

CHAPTER 3

Getting my Act Together

'Mike, you should be in show business, you really should!'

I'd just finished my latest impression and as usual my colleagues, always glad of a bit of light relief during office hours, were highly appreciative. But it was Margaret Fairley who'd spoken. She was always telling me I ought to turn professional and when Margaret spoke I took her seriously because before coming to work in the showroom Margaret had been a Tiller Girl.

I was twenty-one by now and had just failed my driving test yet again, which meant that I still didn't qualify for promotion to rep and the higher pay that went with it. I was getting desperate. It was quite obvious to me that unless I thought of something quickly I was going to be stuck in the showroom all my life. I considered Margaret's words. Surely she should know, and if Margaret thought I was good enough to go into show business, perhaps I should give it a try?

Back home I started to put my most popular impressions together in an act. It was no use doing Mr Jacobs or the customers from the showroom which went down so well at work because nobody else would recognise them. Instead, I chose the family favourites: Steptoe and Son, Harry Worth, Macmillan and the Scottish comedian Chick Murray – the impressions my family and friends seemed to enjoy so much.

I worked away in the front room until I'd made up something approaching a routine, and everyone was encouraging. I was at least as good as the amateurs who stood up to do a turn at Dad's works' social club, they said; why didn't I give it a try?

I knew that if I was serious about going into show business I'd have to face an audience some time. Yet the prospect filled me with dread because of my shyness. I was also getting more and more frustrated at not being able to fulfil my ambitions.

But even I had no idea just how frustrated I was getting at work until the day I bought a detachable collar.

Tommy Dunbar always wore a stiff white detachable collar at the Raincoat Company and for some reason I decided that I must have one too. So during the week I bought myself a collar and a white shirt to go with it and on Friday night I went upstairs to practise putting it on. I had no idea it would be so difficult. If I got the back fixed, the front flew out and if I got the front secured, the back came off.

I don't know how long I wrestled with the damn thing but in the end I lost my temper. I tore off the collar, tore off the shirt and ripped it into shreds and when I'd finished I burst into tears. I wept and wept until eventually my mother came up to see what was wrong.

'What on earth's the matter, Michael? Why are you so upset?' she asked, putting her head round the door.

'I can't get this bloody collar on!' I'd intended to say, but for some reason it came out as, 'I want to go into show business!'

I think I was as surprised as she was by my answer.

'Oh well, love, you'll have to forget about that,' she said gently. 'You'd be hopeless at that.'

'But it's all I want to do,' I insisted.

My mother sat down on the bed and we talked it over. She wasn't happy about the idea because she believed that people in show business lived highly immoral lives but when she saw how serious I was she said, 'Well if you really want to go into show business I suppose you'd better give it a try.'

I think she was worried that I'd be led astray and also that I'd get hurt because she felt I was far too shy to go on the stage, but nevertheless she supported me. She went downstairs and had a word with my father. Knowing Mum she probably said 'He wants to go on the stage. Can't you do something?'

What could my father do? He was a fitter in an engineering works, but he promised to make some enquiries.

It was then that I had two pieces of luck. I met Wilf Fielding and Roy Mayoh. Wilf came first. He was the friend of a work mate who thought we ought to meet each other because of our mutual interest in entertainment. Wilf was actually a business-man with an asphalt company, but in his spare time he was totally star struck and devoted to show business. As soon as he discovered how keen I was to go on the stage he did everything he could to help me. He listened to my act, drove me round the clubs to watch other comics work and was full of enthusiasm whenever I got disheartened.

But Wilf knew we weren't getting anywhere and when he discovered that his secretary, Linda, was going out with a cameraman from ABC television (now Thames) he decided to milk the contact for all it was worth. He persuaded Linda to introduce him to her boyfriend, Roy Mayoh, and then he persuaded Roy to have a look at my act.

We didn't realise then just how lucky we were. Roy Mayoh wasn't just a cameraman. He also wrote scripts for *Crackerjack*, the popular children's programme, and for various comics including Mike and Bernie Winters. In addition, although he'd never been a performer himself he had a natural flair for bringing out the best in other performers. So much so that he went on to become a TV director.

Roy told Wilf to bring me round to his home in Didsbury one evening and there, in his front room, I ran through my impressions. I was obviously very raw and lacking in technique but fortunately Roy seemed to think I had potential.

At that time there were practically no other impressionists about. A few years earlier I'd heard one or two on the radio; a man who did the Duke of Windsor, Peter Cavanagh, a brilliant impersonator who was known as 'the voice of them all' and a man named Peter Goodwright, but lately I hadn't heard much of any of them.

I was a novelty which was a point in my favour. Roy was also struck by the fact that I could do faces. Until then impressionists concentrated mainly on the voices, which was all that was necessary for radio, but with television becoming more and more dominant Roy could see all that would have to change. Finally he was fascinated by the fact that I liked to do political figures, something that was unheard of at the time.

I'd always been interested in politics. Even as a child I liked listening to broadcasts from the House of Commons and since everyone I saw or heard was material for an impression it was only natural that I should do politicians as well as TV personalities.

That is, it seemed only natural to me, but to other people the idea of someone impersonating the prime minister was quite extraordinary.

Roy said he thought I had a chance and he'd be prepared to help me if I was willing to work hard. He didn't need to ask. The one thing I could do was work.

Soon all our spare time was spent either in my parents' front room or Roy's front room, working up my impressions into a proper act.

I had no idea how to work with a microphone, so one

evening Roy turned up with his mother's Ewbank carpet sweeper which he stood upright in front of me.

'Right,' he said, 'that's the mike,' and from then on I had to perform my act into the Ewbank.

Such a feature of my early days was that Ewbank that now Roy's mother keeps it wrapped in brown paper in her loft refusing to part with it for anything and bringing it out on special occasions to show to visitors.

Impressions came easily to me but Roy made me practise the faces over and over in a mirror so that I could see at once the difference made by the fractional lift of an eyebrow, the downward tilt of my mouth. He also taught me how to walk on and off stage, how to play to TV cameras and how to discipline myself to stick to the script no matter what.

I've lost count of the number of hours we put in, Roy watching me intently and yelling now and then, while his long-suffering girlfriend Linda sat in the corner. When they'd gone I'd run through the whole thing yet again. I practised and practised.

This single-minded dedication worried my mother.

'You're working him too hard,' she used to complain to Roy, but Roy always shook his head.

'Nonsense, it's good for him. I'll take him as far as the Royal Command Performance and then I'll be no use to him.'

He said it jokingly and we used to laugh, but as it turned out Roy was as good as his word.

While all this was going on my father was quietly making enquiries as he'd promised. He heard about a man at his works who used to sing in a pub in Dukinfield, Cheshire. Dad got talking to this Frank Riley the next time he saw him and explained about my show business ambitions. How did a young lad get started? he wanted to know. Frank promised to keep an eye out for opportunities and not long afterwards he came up with an idea.

My mother and father, Bridget and Wilf Yarwood, in 1936. They got married two years later.

Me (aged two) and my sister Josephine (aged four).

My sister Josephine (aged ten) and me (aged eight).

Below left: My mother and me (aged fourteen) at Romiley Show.

Below right: My first ever photo session, wearing the suit
Wilf Fielding bought me. I used this picture to
practise writing my autograph.

Early characterisations of Harry Worth (above), Wilfred Brambell's
Steptoe (above right) and Malcolm Muggeridge (below).

My first summer season at the Royal Aquarium Theatre,
Great Yarmouth in 1964. Though my name was at the
bottom of the bill it was still large enough for me!

Fulfilling my most cherished ambition – appearing at the London Palladium.

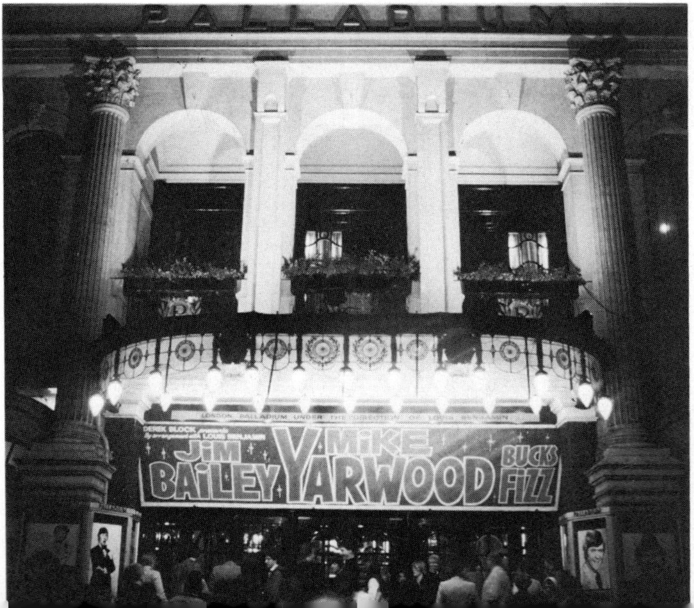

Meeting the Queen at my first Royal Variety Performance in 1968.

Playing football in 1968 with Mike and Bernie Winters.
I was appearing with them at the North Pier in Blackpool at the time.

Our wedding, on 8 November, 1969.

Our first house, Old Dunbar in Prestbury, Cheshire.

Sandra, me and the girls in 1972 (I'm now beginning to form my own chorus line). From the looks on our faces you can tell we hate photo sessions.

This is your Life: Eamonn Andrews escorting me to the Thames Television studios after meeting me outside the Hilton Hotel.

Meeting Prince Charles before his initiation into the Grand Order of Water Rats in 1975.

Outside Buckingham Palace with the family after the investiture of the OBE in 1976.

Me in August 1981 with Charlotte, Clare and my niece Sarah in the middle, at Prestbury House.

Prestbury House in December 1981. I took this photo myself!

'Michael,' said Dad suddenly one evening as we were eating our tea, 'there's a fella I work with who sings in a pub where there's a talent competition on Thursdays. He says you're to go along this Thursday and they'll put you on.'

It was short notice but I got in touch with Wilf and Roy and on Thursday night we presented ourselves at the Albion in Dukinfield. At the last minute I got a serious attack of nerves and Wilf practically had to drag me on stage, but I went out there and did my act, even though my hands were shaking so much I could hardly hold the microphone. I only did three or four minutes but there were quite a few laughs and the applause was generous.

I didn't win, but I came third, which wasn't brilliant since there were only about half a dozen of us in the contest, though I thought it was wonderful. It gave me so much confidence that I decided to go back the following week and enter again.

This time I came second and won 12s 6d.

Wilf and I were delighted and went up to the bar to spend my winnings on a celebratory drink.

'Mike Yarwood, wasn't it?'

I looked round. There was a man propped beside me with a pint of beer in his hand.

'Yes, that's me,' I said, proud to be recognised.

'I'm from the Salvage Hotel, Collyhurst and I'm always looking out for new acts. I'd like to put you on at my place next Friday.'

I was too astonished to reply.

'I'll give you two spots, thirty bob the night,' he went on.

Wilf was nudging me and nodding but all I could think was that thirty bob was too much. I worked all day Saturday at the shop for thirty shillings and now I was being offered the same amount for a few minutes on stage.

'Oh no, that's too much,' I said. (I've never been shrewd!) 'Give me a pound.'

'No,' said the man, 'thirty bob's the going rate.'

'Look, I haven't really got an act; I've only just started doing this,' I insisted and went on to try and knock him down. In the end we agreed to see how it went and sort out the money afterwards, and Wilf and I left the Albion that night with my first booking firmly secured. I felt as high as a kite. I was on my way at last.

Since I was being paid for this appearance I was anxious to give them their money's worth and I decided to improve my props. Roy discouraged me from using too much costume and I tended to rely on the hats I'd been collecting since childhood to help establish each different character. During Friday lunch hour I rushed out and bought a few more. I went to Dunns for a 'Harry Worth' hat, a Hancock trilby and a black homburg for Steptoe. It was a shame about the homburg. There it was all smart and new and I had to sit on it and dirty it to make it look like Steptoe's battered old hat.

The act was quite simple. My hats in a large holdall sat on the table behind me; I told a few gags then took out a hat, put it on my head and did an impression of the person to whom it belonged.

There didn't seem much to it for a pound, let alone thirty bob, but that evening at the Salvage Hotel it went down very well. So well in fact that when the owner handed me thirty bob I didn't feel bad about taking it.

Soon other pubs and working men's clubs started making enquiries, but you couldn't get delusions of grandeur. I was booked for a couple of nights at the Yew Tree Inn in Wythenshawe run by Frank Tansey who was renowned for giving new acts a chance. The second night when I'd finished my spot I asked one of the other comics where you went for your money.

'Oh, you go to the bar,' he said. 'They just give you the money out of the till.'

So I went to the bar which was pretty crowded and waited my turn to be served.

'Yes?' said the barman at last.

'I've come for my money,' I said, almost whispering.

'What name is it?'

That's the impact I'd made there.

'Yarwood,' I said, a bit embarrassed. 'Mike Yarwood.'

He got out a little book, ran his finger down the page and found my name.

'Frank!' he yelled at the top of his voice to where Tansey stood at the other end of the long bar. 'Could you give me £5 for Mike Yarwood?'

And trying not to blush in front of all the curious drinkers who now knew exactly how much I was paid, I collected my money and hurried away.

Not long afterwards I went for an audition at The Richmond in Macclesfield. Nothing came of it but while I was there I met the resident comedian, a young Liverpool comic named Jimmy Tarbuck. It was the early 1960s, the Beatles were the biggest thing ever heard of and anybody from Liverpool was a hot property. So much so that I even thought of pretending to come from Liverpool myself!

Anyway, I discovered that Jimmy had also played the Yew Tree. We got talking and during the conversation he mentioned that he was a full-time comic.

I couldn't believe it.

'You mean you haven't got a job during the day?' I asked.

'No,' he said, 'this is it for me.'

That set me thinking. Wouldn't it be wonderful to give up my job at the showroom (which was getting more and more difficult with all the late nights I was keeping) and do that too.

The next day at work I told Margaret that I'd met a full-time comic and I'd realised that I wanted to be one as well.

'So you're really serious about this, Michael?' she asked.

'Oh yes,' I replied.

She didn't say much to me at the time but she obviously went home and told her husband Bill, who played sax in the band at the Cabaret Club in Manchester, because a few days later she came in and said, 'Bill's got you an audition.'

Apparently the resident compere was leaving and they were looking for a replacement. I'd been to the Cabaret Club with Wilf and I knew what the compere did: he told gags and introduced other acts. It didn't seem too difficult and I thought it would be marvellous to get the job. It was quite a chic place with a glass door and proper food, not chicken in the basket, and best of all it was guaranteed, full-time, all the year round work in show business. I desperately wanted to be offered that job.

Bill explained that I'd need a smart suit for the audition and that was my first problem. I'd outgrown my Italian box by now and I hadn't yet bought a replacement. In the end my uncle came to the rescue and lent me his smartest suit. I was still very skinny and my uncle was quite a lot larger than me, but I didn't think it would matter that the suit was a bit big.

In fact it was very big. I could flap the front like a tent, the sleeves fell down over my hands and the trousers were so long I had to turn them over at the top to avoid treading on the bottoms when I walked. Yes, I had to admit the suit was a bit big on me, but it was a smart suit and I thought that was what counted.

I don't know what they made of my appearance at the club, but they sat through my audition. It was a so-so audition. Not particularly good but not terrible and afterwards they said they were asking candidates to come back and work for one night to see how they fared.

'Have you got a tuxedo?' asked the manager, eyeing my baggy suit. I hadn't.

'Yes he has,' said Wilf quickly.

'Well see that he wears it.'

'Wilf,' I said as soon as we got outside, 'you know I haven't got a dinner suit. I haven't even got an ordinary suit.'

'Yes, but you soon will,' he said and took me out the very next day and bought me my first dinner suit. He wouldn't hear of me paying him back. And if you're reading this, Wilf, I still haven't got the money.

When the big night came I was nervous of course but quite happy – until they mentioned that before I went on stage I had to stand at the door as people were coming in and welcome them like a host. This bothered me very much. Even though I worked in a shop and dealt with customers all day, the thought of greeting the public at the door was much much worse than the thought of giving a performance.

Well, I got through the evening somehow. I mumbled a few words as the people came in, and when it was my turn to take the stage I based my performance on that of the previous compere. I confined myself to telling gags with just a couple of impressions thrown in, and I got a few laughs.

But whatever I did, it obviously wasn't good enough. Whether it was the act or my hopelessness as a host I never knew, but I didn't get the job. I was heartbroken. In twenty-five years in show business I can definitely say that that has been my greatest disappointment.

Yet upset as I was, I still thought the people in the audience that night might recognise me. After all, the club held about 250 people: surely some of them must be on the streets of Manchester in the lunch hour? I strolled around, watching passers-by from under my eyelashes, just as a few years before after scoring my two corners with Bredbury Amateurs, I'd walked around Bredbury wondering if people recognised me. In those days I thought they'd have been telling each other, 'There's the lad who scored two goals', now I thought they must be saying, 'There's the compere from the Cabaret Club.'

Back home I worked harder than ever with Roy, and the bookings continued to come in. A whole new world was opening up – and it was one which horrified my mother.

One evening I turned up to do my act and discovered it was a stag night, complete with stripper. Comics hated doing stag nights because it was impossible to follow a stripper. Most of them were so terrified that they'd come out with as many four-letter words as they could think of and they showed their approval of the girls by lewd gestures. Left to myself I might have fallen into the same trap, but Roy said, 'I never want to see you doing anything like that. Just do your normal act. Die if you have to, but don't sink to that level.'

Nervously repeating his words I headed for the dressing room, opened the door and found myself looking at a naked woman.

'Come in, love. We're sharing,' said the stripper quite nonchalantly and carried on sticking tassels to her nipples.

I was still at the age where I'd stare at a naked woman and I was getting all hot under the collar trying not to look. I turned away and fiddled with my tie, but the stripper seemed unaware of my embarrassment.

'Here, could you help me, love?' she asked suddenly. 'I've got to put these tassels on my bottom and I can't get it right. Can you stick them dead centre for me?'

Hands trembling I somehow managed to fix the tassels where she'd indicated. She looked over her shoulder, and gave her bottom a twitch to set the tassels going.

'Yes, that's fine. Thanks,' she said and, collecting the rest of her gear, she headed for the stage.

As time went on of course, I got quite used to the strippers. They looked tarty but they took their work seriously and it was just a living for them. However, you never got the chance to have a proper conversation with a stripper. They worked at four or five clubs a night and they didn't hang around. As soon as they'd finished the strip they were off to the next place.

And it wasn't too bad for me to follow a stripper. The audience might be restless at first but I finished with Steptoe and Son, turning from side to side and switching hats as the dialogue went back and forth between father and son. Since the series was at the height of its popularity, this always went extremely well.

I had an advantage over other comics. They only had themselves to win over an audience, but I had Tony Hancock, Chick Murray and Steptoe and Son, some of the finest names in the country to help me.

By the time my fortnight's holiday from work came round a few weeks later, my show business career was really snowballing. I didn't want to miss any bookings so I stayed at home and rested during the day that year, but while I was away from work I got an offer for a whole week, doubling at two clubs for £30. No sooner had I accepted than I got another offer of £30.

I couldn't believe it. My wages at the showroom, plus the thirty bob from my Saturday job, brought me in about £12 a week and now I was being offered £60 – five times as much. It didn't mean I'd earn £60 every week, of course, but if Jimmy Tarbuck could manage without a daytime job, I began to think surely I could do it too.

I mentioned to my mother that I was thinking of giving up my job and turning professional.

'Well, why not,' she said. 'You can always get another job if it doesn't work out.'

So I phoned the showroom and told my boss that I wasn't coming back.

To my surprise he was delighted. Absolutely over the moon. It wasn't very flattering!

'Well, Michael, I wish you all the luck in the world,' he said. 'I hope you become a big star one day.'

'I'll come in and pick up my cards, shall I?'

'Oh no, no,' he said hastily. 'That's quite all right. We'll send them to you, don't worry.'

I think he was afraid that if I came back I might change my mind.

There was no chance of that, of course. I was in the money now and one of the first things I did was to buy myself a good suit. It was the start of what was to become my habitual extravagance. Admittedly Roy had always stressed the importance of looking good on stage, but I didn't need much persuading. An off-the-peg suit wasn't good enough for me; oh no, my suit had to be tailor-made.

I went to a tailor in Stockport and ordered a lovely kid mohair suit for £65, which was a great deal of money in the early 1960s. It was beautiful; shiny and soft and very fashionable. I thought I was the bees' knees in that suit.

Roy was right about looking good on stage of course, but really some of the places I played in those days weren't good enough for my kid mohair. There were beer halls where you had to shout to make yourself heard, where people wandered back and forth to the bar, bellowing orders across the crowded room while you were doing your act, and sometimes fights broke out. It was terrible.

Yet I was going up in the world. At last Roy got me my first week's engagement at a proper nightclub in Manchester – not a working men's club but a posh night club called The Ponderosa.

The first night was a very big occasion for me, made even more nerve-racking by the fact that Roy had invited along Billy Scott from ABC Television's entertainment department in the hope that he might get me a TV audition.

My legs were shaking, my hands were shaking and at a crucial moment in my act a waiter called out loudly 'Chicken in the basket!'

Roy had always insisted that no matter what happened I should stick to the script and plough on, so I did. But when I came to the new section of the act, a series of fast, visual gags, I almost came unstuck. I was supposed to pinch out the skin on both sides of my neck while saying: 'Excuse me waiter, I've swallowed my spoon.'

I managed the line well enough but my hands were trembling so much I couldn't pull out my neck. The audience must have been puzzled but Roy laughed and laughed. He thought it was the funniest part of the whole evening.

Despite the problems, Billy Scott got me an audition at ABC and as a result I was invited to do a warm-up for a programme called *Comedy Bandbox*. This was a popular show which mixed established comedians like Arthur Askey and Ted Ray with newcomers. You didn't actually appear on screen when you were booked as a warm-up artist, you simply appeared first and got the audience in the mood for the rest of the performers. But it was understood that if you did well at the warm-up you were likely to be invited to appear on the programme.

I knew that Jimmy Tarbuck, who had by now become a friend, had been on the warm-up one week, the show the next and on the strength of his success had been invited to appear on *Sunday Night at the London Palladium* – the top TV programme of the time.

This could be my big break. As usual I was very, very nervous but my act went down very well. It was marvellous to work with an audience who sat quietly and listened to you, and who wanted to laugh. Soon I found I was enjoying myself and I finished to loud applause.

Afterwards Peter Dulay, the producer, who later went on to make *Candid Camera*, told me that he liked my work and wanted to book me for next week's show.

I was over the moon. I'd promised I would let my mother know the outcome as soon as possible so I dashed out to the call box outside the studios and phoned her. But I've always loved playing practical jokes and I couldn't resist having a little fun.

'Sorry, Mum,' I said, sounding disappointed, 'nothing came of it.'

My mother was immediately reassuring. 'Never mind, love, there'll be another time.'

But I couldn't keep it up. 'No, I'm only kidding,' I laughed, 'I'm on next week!'

When I got home very late that night after a celebratory meal, there was a large piece of paper propped on my pillow. 'Congratulations. Goodnight, God Bless. Mum.'

CHAPTER 4

On my Way

My first *Comedy Bandbox* was screened on 21 December, 1963 and I think my parents were even more excited about it than I was. Before the show my mother was so nervous that she felt compelled to clean the oven with particular thoroughness and she was only able to watch my debut from around the oven door. My father's not one to show his feelings, but I'm told that throughout the performance the back of his neck and his ears went bright pink with pleasure.

I was on a high for several days afterwards. This was it, I thought. I was on my way to stardom now. I'd watched Jimmy Tarbuck's career with amazement. He had appeared at the Palladium on the Sunday night and on the Monday morning he was a star. It was literally an overnight success, and I thought the same thing would happen to me. But it didn't.

After *Comedy Bandbox* I waited for the Palladium to call. They didn't. Nothing happened, and my life went on much the same as before. I was disappointed. I was *very* disappointed actually. In fact I felt extremely jealous of Jimmy. I've never been as jealous about anything as I was about Jimmy Tarbuck at that time.

But the bookings were coming in and now I was able to command a higher fee because I could be billed 'as seen on TV'. Life was certainly varied. On one occasion I was booked to double for a week at the Cabaret Club, Hanley and then afterwards at a country restaurant called The Vicarage. With me on the bill were two gorgeous girls called Angela Bracewell (who'd become famous as a hostess for Bruce Forsyth on *Beat the Clock* at the Palladium) and Janet Mahoney, who had a glamorous singing double act.

The week went smoothly enough until the Wednesday. I might have known it was going to be one of those nights when I arrived to find that it was also a wrestling evening and we were expected to perform in the wrestling ring. It wasn't too bad for me, but the sight of those two girls with their blonde hair piled up and their tight, ankle-length sequined gowns trying to climb over the ropes – well, it was the most bizarre thing I'd ever seen in my life.

Afterwards we dashed out to get our lift over to The Vicarage and discovered that a thick fog had come down, a real pea-souper. The journey was a bit hair-raising but we made it all right. Unfortunately most of the customers hadn't. The restaurant, a nice oak-beamed place which seated about 100 people, that night contained only four, all seated at one table.

The manager met me in the bar.

'Forget it,' he said.

If anyone said that to me today I would say fine, terrific, but I was very, very keen in those days.

'I'd rather go on,' I assured him.

'It's all right, you'll be paid. I'm not asking you to take less money,' he said. 'It's just that I don't think it's worth it for four people, do you?'

'Yes, I don't mind that. I must go on,' I insisted, and that performance has since gone down in my personal book of records as the smallest audience I've played to as a professional.

It wasn't too bad. All the staff came out of the kitchen and the cocktail bar and gathered about the four customers, and I virtually stood at the table and went through my act.

There was a terrific response, half appreciation and half sympathy, and I was glad I'd gone through with it. I felt a real professional.

Angela and Janet, following my example, ran through their act too, then we were off again for our last stop of the night, the motorway service station where we ate bacon and eggs after the show.

By this time I was enjoying myself very much and I didn't want to go home. The girls were gorgeous and I didn't feel like leaving them. Outside the fog was still very dense and travelling was difficult, so although I could have arranged a lift home instead I made the weather an excuse and said I'd have to stay at the girls' hotel, which was in Newcastle under Lyme, not far away.

I went back with the girls, feeling pleased with myself because I'd been hanging around them all week, but my sophistication crumbled in the face of the night porter.

'Sorry,' he said, 'we've got no rooms vacant.'

'Not even one single?'

He shook his head.

It was four o'clock in the morning, I was a long way from home and I was getting desperate.

'Couldn't I sleep in the lounge? I'd pay for it.'

'Certainly not.'

Behind me Angela and Janet exchanged glances.

'Mike,' said Angela, drawing me aside, 'there are three beds in our room. You can stay there with us but you'll have to get out early in the morning before the chambermaid comes round or they'll think something's going on.'

Looking back I think they were very shy about the whole thing. We all were. I spent the rest of the night sleeping in my clothes on top of the spare bed and before seven I crept out of the hotel.

It was very cold and there's not a lot to do in Newcastle under Lyme at seven in the morning. I found a transport café which was open, bought a cup of coffee and made it last. There was no alternative because I'd run out of money. I lingered as long as I dared, then I went out and wandered around looking in shop windows. I was wearing a thin coat and sweater and for some reason the black patent shoes from my dinner suit. I was cold, my feet hurt and I was very, very tired. But it could have been worse. I could have been wearing my full dinner suit!

Eventually, as soon as I decently could, I went back to the hotel to see if the girls were up and whether they could lend me some money. They were still in bed but Angela kindly came down and gave me a pound. (You could do something with a pound in those days.)

I went back to the transport café and had a meal. Then I caught the bus to Hanley so that I would be ready for the club in the evening, and went to the cinema for a sleep. There was a war picture on which was bound to do the trick because I've never been a great fan of war pictures. I'm not one for a lot of action. I like good dialogue.

Unfortunately this wasn't just any old war film. It was *The Great Escape*. It was so good I didn't get a wink of sleep even though I sat through it twice to kill time. I loved it, but when I came out of the cinema I was more tired than ever and I still had two shows to do.

I think that was the longest day of my life.

Despite my experience in Newcastle under Lyme, I was still very disorganised about finding accommodation. I remember accepting a booking for a week in Leeds and it was only after

I'd finished my act on the first night that I realised I didn't have a place to stay and it was after eleven o'clock.

'D'you know where I can stay tonight?' I asked one of the other comics. 'Can you recommend anywhere?'

'I don't think you'll get anything now,' he said. 'But I've seen Mrs So-and-so in the audience. She puts up all the pros, and might be able to help you.'

Mrs So-and-so was sitting with a group of people when I went over.

'Well,' she said when I explained the problem, 'you'll have to share with this gentleman here tonight, but the rest of the week you'll have the room to yourself.'

When she said share, I didn't realise she meant share the bed. The 'other gentleman' (a rep) and I were to share a double bed. In fact we weren't too bothered: we were both straight so there was no problem.

The next morning he left and I had the room to myself. The house seemed to be a lucky find. It was large and comfortably furnished and there were good cooked breakfasts every morning. There seemed to be a lot of people staying there, particularly girls. The phone never stopped ringing, but I wasn't surprised it was popular. The only slight irritation was that sometimes you would have to vacate your room for an hour or so. I would be resting in the afternoon and Mrs So-and-so would tap on the door.

'Excuse me. Would you mind awfully but one of the girls wants to do a bit of sewing,' she'd ask, and I would have to vacate the room and watch television downstairs.

It was Thursday before I realised what was going on. I opened a cupboard and found a riding whip, then I opened a drawer and saw a pile of contraceptives. I was staying in a brothel!

When it came to a trip to London though, my mother had a hand in the arrangements. It always impressed club owners to say you'd played London so when I was booked by a southern agent for a week at a place called the Caribbean Club in the Edgware Road I was thrilled. I'd never been to London before but my mother, convinced that the capital was a den of iniquity, asked my uncle in Swiss Cottage if I could stay with him for the week.

Roy Mayoh still tried to accompany me to important bookings whenever he could, but that particular week he couldn't get away. I was on my own.

I didn't like London. It was so big and fast, and I felt lost, lonely and very frightened. My rehearsal at the Caribbean Club didn't help. The place turned out to be a small, dimly lit restaurant, so intimate that you didn't need a microphone and the staff didn't even smile as I went through my act. I got the impression that they couldn't understand my northern accent and that London audiences would be impossible to get through to.

Back at my uncle's I grew more and more nervous and the upshot was that I didn't turn up at the club that night. I set off but I couldn't go through with it. I walked straight past the club and went into the nearest pub instead where I sat all night over a couple of pints of beer.

Later I phoned my parents and told them what had happened.

'I'm not going back,' I said to my mother.

'No, of course not,' she said sympathetically. 'You don't have to if you don't want to. Come home if you're not happy.'

But in the background I could hear my father saying, 'Tell him not to be so silly. Tell him to get back on there ... I'm going to phone Roy Mayoh.'

The next morning I was summoned to the agent's office. He was furious.

'You didn't turn up!' he snapped.

I tried to explain why, but he cut me short.

'What did you do before you came into show business?'

'I sold clothing,' I said.

'Well, I should go back to doing that if I were you. You won't work for me again.'

Miserably I returned to Swiss Cottage to find Roy Mayoh on the phone. He gave me a real earful.

'Right,' he said finally, 'you go back to that club and you tell them you'll work the rest of the week for nothing.'

It took a lot of courage but I went back, walked in and the owner, a big, warm Greek, was absolutely marvellous. He let me finish the week and he insisted on paying me too.

As it turned out my fears were unjustified. The audience seemed to understand my accent, they laughed in the right places and the act seemed to go well. But there were other hazards to being at the hub of things.

I've always enjoyed doing topical gags and this was the time of Harold Macmillan and the notorious Christine Keeler.

'Harold Macmillan has always said you've never had it so good,' I said to the audience one night, 'but since Christine Keeler's arrived he says you've never had it so often...

'Actually Christine Keeler's been signed to play for Spurs – because she plays in any position...'

I paused before the next gag and as I did so the door opened and in walked an attractive woman accompanied by a powerful-looking man. It was Christine Keeler with a friend. I toned the act down after that.

Other bookings in London followed my appearance at the Caribbean, and I was learning all the time. Like other comics I tried to silence hecklers as quickly as possible and one night in Soho a woman in the audience started having a go at me. She went on and on and in the end I said something I'd heard an American comic say.

'Be fair, madam,' I pleaded, 'I've only got half an hour to earn my living. You've got all night.'

We were in Soho, an area renowned for prostitution, and it got a fair laugh, but afterwards I was invited to the woman's table.

'Sit down and have a drink with us,' said her husband.

'Er well, thank you but no.'

'*Yes*,' he said. He was a big man.

'All right. I'll have a gin and bitter lemon,' I said, hastily sitting down.

And to my horror he ordered me a whole bottle of gin and a small bottle of bitter lemon to go with it. So there I was with this bottle of gin all to myself, desperately looking for a polite way to get rid of it. It was some time before I managed to make my escape, leaving behind the bottle still more than three-quarters full.

Around the same time I also learned the dangers of making fun of members of the audience. In those days in the clubs it was normal to try and get a laugh out of anybody who moved and the ad libs weren't very tasteful. Anyway, this particular night a man got up and went to the toilet and I thought I would get him when he came back. A few minutes later he reappeared and I said, 'I know where you've been and I'll tell you something else – you missed. Your shoes are wet.'

He just stared at me, then walked straight past his seat and came over to where I was standing. He kept on coming until he was just a few inches away and I was sure he was going to hit me. Then he stopped, took off his shoe and wiped it on my jacket.

There was no way I could top that. I was finished. That's one up to you, I thought, and was more wary of ad libs in future.

But despite London and the posh nightclubs a substantial part of my living in those days was made in the working men's clubs. Roy, Wilf and I particularly enjoyed the Yorkshire clubs because of the concert chairmen.

Each club had a chairman who booked the acts and ran the entertainment. During the evening they sat in a pulpit affair with a little door in it and a bell on top. They rang the bell for order when the audience got restless, even if this happened in the middle of an act. Ping went the bell, cutting across the song or joke, followed by the loud command of 'Give order!'

I'm told a concert chairman once interrupted a girl singer who was dying a death with, 'Order. Give order. Give this poor cow a chance.'

They also introduced the acts, first blowing down the microphone, and I was once announced like this:

'Ladies and gentlemen, we've got this young fella coming on who was on *Comedy Bandbox*. Now I'm only prepared to pay him £6 but he wanted £8. Anyway, he's quite good so I've picked £2 out of my own pocket to get him here tonight. Here he is – Mike Yarwood!'

Yes, the concert chairmen were wonderful characters, so good in fact that Roy and I decided to introduce one into my act. 'Tommy' was the first invented character I'd ever used in public. He had a limp and a flat cap and he picked wax out of his ears as he talked.

'Right, shut your holes,' he would tell the audience, first blowing vigorously down the microphone to check that it was working.

Tommy became a very strong part of my act and he was surprisingly popular with the concert chairmen themselves. They all thought he was based on a chairman at the club up the road. No matter where I was, it was always the club up the road!

Yet the real concert chairmen were funnier than anything I could invent. I remember one Sunday lunchtime booking at the Greaseborough Social Club in Rotherham, the most prestigious working men's club of them all. Dickie Valentine was top of the bill, I was second top because I'd been on television, and there were about four or five acts in all.

Dickie and I were on last of course, and we were chatting in the dressing room when the concert chairman came in.

'Can you keep your act short,' he said to me, 'because it's nearly two o'clock and they like to leave at five past two to catch the two-fifteen bus. So keep it brief.'

'OK,' I said. 'When d'you think I'll be on?'

'You should be on in about five minutes,' he replied.

He was just walking out of the door when Dickie Valentine, top of the bill and the star of the show said, 'Hang on a minute. What time will I be on?'

'Oh,' said the chairman. 'We might not get to you.'

As it turned out they did get to Dickie, but in the middle of his rendering of 'Climb Every Mountain', practically the entire audience got up and filed out.

I was sitting at the artists' table at the side and I started to laugh. In the end I was crying with laughter and Dickie, who'd been trying to finish the song, had to abandon the attempt because he was laughing so much too.

Every time I saw Dickie after that I said, 'They might not get to you...!'

There were so many concert chairman stories that were supposed to be true. Like the one about the ventriloquist who went on for his first spot and didn't get any laughs.

'That didn't go down very well,' he said to the concert chairman afterwards.

'They can't hear you; it's a very big room,' said the concert chairman. 'Put the dummy nearer the microphone next time.'

But the concert chairmen weren't always figures of fun. At a lot of clubs they liked you to split your act into four or five three-minute spots and if you died in the first spot you knew you had to go back out and die again at intervals throughout the evening.

Some comics hated it so much that I've actually seen them climbing out of the windows to get away without having to face the concert chairman.

I heard about some places where they didn't applaud at all. They showed their appreciation by putting their hands up, as if they were casting a vote, and some poor unsuspecting artists would finish their acts to complete silence and look into the room to see a forest of arms. I never experienced that, thank goodness.

Looking back I can't say I had a tough time in the clubs, not like some entertainers. My only real regret was that my mother hardly saw me 'live' at all.

Shortly after I started work she had a 'bad day' that lasted far longer than twenty-four hours.

It all started at the hairdressers'. She went regularly to have her hair done without mishap, but on this particular day she suddenly felt 'funny' under the hairdryer. She was so bad that they sent her home in a taxi and she went straight to bed.

There she stayed for several weeks, unable to describe what was wrong. 'I just feel terrible,' she kept saying, and there was nothing we could do for her.

In the end my father had to send for Josephine who was away at a nurses' training college. She postponed her exams to look after Mum, and Dad and I tiptoed round helping out where we could.

My mother recovered after a while but she suffered from a form of agoraphobia in varying degrees from then on. The idea of going to a nightclub was too much for her. Roy once persuaded her to come to see me but she only stayed a few minutes. The crowds and the noise made her panic and she had to leave. It was such a shame because she wanted to see my act, but she had to be content with watching it on the television and with my blow by blow accounts over the telephone afterwards.

CHAPTER 5

Impossible Dreams
come True

I spotted the poster right away. I was waiting in my agent's office and there it was staring me in the face: 'The Bob Monkhouse Show, Central Pier, Blackpool'.

Central Pier, Blackpool – the very name spelled glamour to me. It was there that I'd dreamed my impossible dreams of show business when I was on holiday as a child.

Morecambe and Wise had appeared at the Central Pier; so had Ken Dodd, Eddie Calvert and countless other big names. An appearance there was known as a stepping stone to greater things, and I badly wanted that.

'Dave,' I said, pointing to the poster when my agent appeared, 'I'd love to be in that show.'

'Well, I can't promise anything,' said Dave Forrester, 'but I'll see what I can do.'

My career was progressing fast. The previous year, 1964, I'd been introduced to the delights of working a summer season with an eighteen-week run in Great Yarmouth.

Billy Fury was top of the bill with Rolf Harris and Karl Denver in between, and way down at the bottom came Mike Yarwood. Yet when I arrived in Great Yarmouth I couldn't believe how big my name was. Although it was bottom of the bill the bill was enormous! Billy Fury's name was spelled out in letters larger than he was and consequently although mine was a lot smaller it was still the largest it had ever been. Everywhere I went my name seemed to scream out at me.

I rented a flat over a café not far from the theatre.

'I'm sure you'll be comfortable here,' said the landlady. 'Mark Wynter was here last year.' She was besotted with Mark Wynter and brought his name into conversation whenever possible.

Working a summer season was a totally different way of life and I still had a lot to learn. My first night at the theatre, which was a grotty, tatty little place, I was confronted for the first time by stage make-up. I fiddled around with the sticks and colours for a bit but I wasn't getting anywhere.

'What do I do with this pancake 25?' I said at last to the lead dancer with whom I was sharing the dressing room. 'How do I put it on?'

'Well, first you wet the sponge,' he told me.

'Oh I see.' But it was quite obvious that I didn't see because the next moment he took pity on me.

'D'you want me to do it for you to show you what to do?'

I did, so he got to work and in a surprisingly short time I was fully made-up. What I didn't realise however was that dancers wear a great deal more make-up than other artists and he'd made me up like a ballet dancer with big black lines right round my eyes and loads of mascara. I must have looked like Danny La Rue without a frock. I think I got right through the season before someone put me right, and eventually I learned to do it properly.

Summer seasons were sociable affairs. All the acts left the theatre at the same time because they had to hang around for the finale, consequently we all tended to go off to the same place afterwards. In towns where there were several theatres, all the theatricals used to gather together and since our evenings began when the theatres closed, they usually went on till the early hours of the morning.

In Yarmouth there was a place across the road from the theatre called the Savoy Hotel, which despite its name was a small guest house. Everyone gravitated to the Savoy, with the exception of Billy Fury who used to do his act then disappear. I got used to staying up all night and I remember thinking how nice it was to go home at dawn and fall asleep to the sound of birdsong. I can't do it now!

One afternoon as I was leaving for the theatre my landlady stopped me.

'What's your favourite meal?' she asked, because I'd been taking most of my meals in the café.

I thought for a moment. 'I like Indian curry,' I said. I'd been introduced to this exotic dish quite recently after a nightclub booking.

'Right,' she said, 'I'll do you a nice curry.'

I thanked her and went on my way thinking nothing more about it.

A few days later there was a knock on my door at about twelve-thirty in the morning. I was still in bed because I'd been up all night, but I got into my dressing-gown and staggered to the door.

There stood my landlady with a tray of curry, rice and potatoes, 'I've got your favourite!' she said with a beaming smile and put it down on the table in my room. Then she pulled out a chair and sat down to watch me eat it.

Now it may have been lunch-time to most people, but to me it was early breakfast and the powerful smell of the curry was curdling my stomach. But I didn't want to offend my landlady so I sat there and picked at the food until eventually she had to leave.

As a result of the Great Yarmouth show I was invited to

appear with Ken Dodd at the Royal Court Theatre in Liverpool for the Christmas season and Roy, who had his own job to do after all, thought it was about time I had an agent to look after me. He sorted through his contacts and put me in touch with Dave Forrester. So now I had an agent to go with my mohair suit and shortly afterwards I got a car.

This was my idea. I'd seen a pale blue Austin 1100 which I could afford. I still hadn't passed my driving test but everyone said that the best way to pass a driving test was to get plenty of practice and what better way to practise than in your own car? So I bought the Austin for £600 and persuaded a friend to look after it for me.

The best thing about appearing at the Royal Court was working with Ken Dodd. I used to stand in the wings every night watching him – he was incredible. I'd never seen anyone exhaust an audience like he did. Where a good comedian might get one belly laugh every three minutes, Ken got a good laugh every minute. I used to say he machine-gunned an audience. I had such great admiration for him and I'm sure my later impression of Ken Dodd was formed during those evenings in the wings.

I didn't just watch Ken's act, I also hung around him generally. I thought I would learn something from Ken. He was very friendly, always cheerful and he treated everyone the same. He was particularly nice to the public and that impressed me.

Every night he used to sit at the stage door as the public filed in and he signed every autograph. If anyone wanted to come and see him personally about something he would very rarely turn them away, and he once kept Bernard Delfont waiting because he was talking to members of the public.

Ken was renowned for his unpunctuality and the fact that he didn't come off the stage if he was enjoying himself. Before the show the stage-hands used to stand outside the theatre looking down the street and if they could see him they would dash in and say to the orchestra, 'OK, you can start the overture now.'

The music would start and Ken would come running through the stage door into his dressing room. As his special tune began he would fling on his stage clothes like greased lightning then dash out on to the stage in time to open the show, as if he'd been waiting in the wings for hours. He made it every time, but I could never understand how.

The end of the evening was the opposite. Ken's act closed the show and if it was going well he went on and on until the audience was exhausted with laughing. Some nights we would go on for the finale without a set because the stage hands had gone home.

I got good reviews for that show and as a result Dave was able to get me into Bob Monkhouse's show at the Central Pier as I'd requested.

As it turned out we did terrible business. It was a very wet summer which usually helps, but this particular season it didn't seem to make any difference and the theatre was never full. However, the performers had a good time, and we all mucked in together. Most of us did sketches with Bob, and I did a couple. I enjoyed it very much. I had the fun, without the responsibility of being top of the bill. What's more, my new impression of Harold Wilson, now prime minister, was going down very well indeed.

After the show we would gravitate to a certain restaurant in town where the theatricals from all the shows (and there were quite a few) went to eat.

There I met Tommy Cooper and Eric Morecambe, and I seemed to spend the whole night laughing. Funnily enough you didn't ever see Ernie Wise with Eric – they were never together socially.

It was Tommy Cooper who stands out in my mind

particularly at this time. He was such a funny man. He didn't have to do a thing – just the sight of his face made you laugh.

One night in the restaurant I ordered chips and a dish of boiled potatoes arrived. I was a bit disappointed but I was prepared to eat the potatoes rather than make a fuss. Not Tommy. He engineered the situation into a drama and made a big fuss until the waiter came over, then he complained on my behalf.

'I'm very sorry, sir,' said the waiter, turning to me, 'but it's too late to have chips now. The chef has gone. You show business people are always late; you should ring us and let us know you're coming and then we can do chips for you but it's too late now.'

And having wound the whole situation up, Tommy turned innocently to me and said, 'He's right, you know.'

On another occasion I stepped into a lift on the ground floor of a building with four or five other people and Tommy came dashing in just as the doors were closing.

'Hello, Tom,' I said.

'Hello, how's it going?' he asked.

We compared notes about our respective shows, then at the third floor Tommy got out.

'That's the most boring forty-five seconds I've ever spent in my life,' he said and walked away without a backward glance, leaving me with egg on my face in front of the other passengers.

On another occasion I remember standing at a bar with Tommy.

'What are you having?' he asked.

'Half a lager,' I replied.

'Keep your voice down,' he said, hoping no one else in the bar would take advantage of his generosity.

The drinks came along, Tommy handed over a pound note and the barman handed over his change. Tommy counted it carefully.

'Hey, it's two shillings short,' he said.

The barman, clearly irritated, slapped two shilling pieces down on the bar near Tommy's elbow. We finished our drinks, I moved forward to buy another round and Tommy started groping around on the bar.

'Hey, Mike; there were two shillings there, two shilling pieces. They've gone.' He looked up and down the bar, lifting ashtrays and cigarette packets.

'They've gone,' he repeated in disgust. 'I wouldn't mind – it's not the principle, it's the money.'

It's impossible to convey on paper just how comical these incidents were. You had to be there, to see the expression on the face, hear the tone of the voice, to appreciate it.

It was the same with Eric Morecambe. He walked into my dressing room at the theatre one night, sat down and started watching the television.

I started to say something but he shushed me.

'D'you mind? I haven't come to see you, you know; I've come to watch the television.'

He *had* come to see me of course, but that was Eric, and he could reduce you to helpless laughter just by raising an eyebrow.

Yes, I was enjoying myself in Blackpool, but despite all the fun there was only one thing on my mind and that was *Sunday Night at the London Palladium*. Ever since I'd appeared on *Comedy Bandbox* I'd been waiting and hoping and praying for my big chance and it hadn't come. Now the series was drawing to a close for that year and it was beginning to look as if I'd lost my chance. Yet still I hoped.

Then on the Monday before the last show I found a visitor in my dressing room.

'Hello Mike, I'm Alec Fyne from ATV,' he said. 'We would like you to do *Sunday Night at the London Palladium*.'

It was one of the best moments of my life. I'd been hoping

and praying for so long that I couldn't believe it was really happening.

Alec didn't need to ask me twice. I accepted straight away. They wanted me to do about four well-known people and I had a five-minute spot. 'No problem,' I said, although by then my act was about three times as long as that and I'd have to do some drastic pruning.

I talked it over with Roy. He was already well aware of the problem television posed for entertainers. Until it came along an act would virtually last you a lifetime. You could tour the whole country doing the same act because people wouldn't have seen it. Once it's been performed on television, however, that's the end of it. You need a new act.

A lot of entertainers didn't seem to realise that. They went on screen and did a bit of their act, then the next time they did a bit more until eventually they'd used it all up and were left with nothing.

Roy told me I mustn't let that happen to me so I kept my act intact and got a script-writer to write me a script for the Palladium. We used the same characters but different lines.

I was still working at the Central Pier of course, but Sunday was our day off so I flew down to London for the show then flew back again to report to the theatre as usual on Monday night.

I'd never been on an aeroplane before so I was doubly nervous, but fortunately at the airport I bumped into Tommy Cooper who was flying to London and we travelled together. Tommy was even more hysterical than usual and the flight passed in a blur of laughter. I didn't have time to feel frightened.

The Palladium however was a different matter. I was on my own and the place seemed enormous. Just looking at those tiers and tiers of plush seats was enough to make you panic.

I was way down the bill of course so I was put in a tiny

dressing room high up at the back of the building somewhere, and my chief memory is of pacing up and down. I seemed to do this for hours.

There was a rehearsal at eleven o'clock in the morning. Then another, and later on in the afternoon there was a full dress-rehearsal. Then finally at seven-thirty the show started.

The schedule meant that there was a lot of hanging around at the theatre. I don't know what the other performers did to pass the time but I paced up and down, feeling sicker and sicker as the hours crawled by.

The very worst point was when I was standing in the wings trying to control my shaking legs. Out on stage I could hear compere Norman Vaughan say, 'And now here's a fellow who's going to do the prime minister ...'

And I knew there was no turning back then. I had to go through with it.

Hazily I heard the words 'Mike Yarwood!' and stumbled out into the spotlights.

I was lucky that night. It was a super audience. They hadn't paid to come in and they were in a happy mood, ready to have a good time. I think I must have been trembling from head to foot until I got my first laugh and then suddenly I was away. My nerves settled down and I began to enjoy myself. By the time I reached the end of my act I was on a high and I walked off the stage as exhilarated as if I'd had a pep-pill or a couple of large brandies.

As always the first thing I did was to rush to a call box to telephone my parents. My mother had been making cups of tea and scrubbing out the kitchen all day and was now busily attacking the oven because the show was recorded at seven-thirty then shown an hour later. Apparently all our friends and neighbours were gathered round the television and my mother was greatly relieved to hear that everything had gone well. I think she was actually able to watch the show from her chair for a change.

A week later there was a further triumph when I finally passed my driving test. I didn't do too badly with the driving but as usual my knowledge of the highway code let me down. They were very strict about that sort of thing in those days and I sat there waiting apprehensively for the verdict.

'Well, Mr Yarwood,' said the examiner, 'you'll have to brush up on your highway code but I'm going to give you a pass.'

I could have kissed him. I suppose everyone feels the same way when they pass their driving test but it meant so much to me. I'd been waiting for so long and now at last I was free to take to the road in my Austin 1100.

Only one little thing soured that happy time. I got my first taste of the other side of being a celebrity. Of course I wasn't an overnight star like Jimmy Tarbuck, I wasn't even a real celebrity, but in my own little corner of Bredbury I was getting quite well known.

One evening, not long after *Sunday Night at the London Palladium*, I was standing at the bar in the local pub and in walked a man I knew.

'Nice to see you again, Mike,' he said. 'What would you like to drink?'

Now at this time I was drinking brandy and coke which was very fashionable and to my mind a lovely drink. In Bredbury though I knew they wouldn't understand and that I was bound to offend this man.

'No, I'm OK, thanks all the same,' I said.

'No, no, have a drink,' he insisted. He went on and on until eventually I realised there was no way out.

'OK,' I said, 'I'll have a brandy and coke.'

'Brandy and coke? Brandy and coke! Bloody hell, I

remember you when you used to drink a pint of beer. Brandy and coke ...!'

In the end I felt so embarrassed I wished I'd gone somewhere else that evening.

Yet my career was going from strength to strength. Superstitiously I kept thinking well this is it, it can't get any better than this. But it did.

The Palladium show came back with a new format and was retitled *The New Palladium Show*. It was never as prestigious as the old version but I was delighted to be asked to appear and over the next few months I was on it several times. I also started what was to be a long association with the Bachelors who were at the height of their success and made regular tours of the country. The Bachelors liked to have a lot of comedy in their show and after my appearance with them in Coventry I became part of the team.

Between Palladiums and Bachelor shows I also managed to do a summer season in Bournemouth with Harry Worth. That summer of 1966 was one of the nicest summers of my life. I was working with lovely people like Harry, Joe Henderson and Billy Dainty, England won the World Cup and I fell in love for the first time. It was quite a summer.

Harry Worth was the first pleasant surprise. I didn't know quite what to expect from Harry. I'd seen him on television for years: at the time he was one of the most successful comedians after Hancock and he was frequently impersonated on the radio by Peter Cavanagh.

It was quite possible that he wouldn't have time for a newcomer like me, I thought, but I was wrong. Harry turned out to be very much like his screen character.

In Bournemouth the theatricals' restaurant was a little place called The Bistro and one night Harry and I went there for a meal. He ordered minestrone soup, but when it came along Harry realised he didn't have a spoon.

It was a very busy restaurant and it took him some time to attract the waitress's attention.

'Could I have a spoon for this soup?' he asked.

'Oh yes. Just a moment sir,' she said and she went off and didn't come back.

For the next few minutes Harry tried in vain to get a spoon. 'Soup'll get cold if I don't get a spoon in a minute,' he said, failing once again to catch the waitress's eye.

In the end the head waiter came over.

'What's the problem sir?'

'I haven't got a spoon for my soup,' said Harry.

And the waiter just leant forward, lifted the red paper napkin at the side of Harry's plate and there beneath it lay the soup spoon.

'Oh, ho ho, I didn't see it under the napkin,' said Harry with egg all over his face, but I don't think he was too embarrassed. Things like that happened to Harry all the time.

Life was full of surprises. One day we discovered that we'd both just started to play golf.

'Let's go and have a game,' said Harry, so we set off in his car, but he couldn't find the golf course and very soon we got hopelessly lost.

Finally, well after midday we came to an attractive restaurant so we abandoned the idea of golf and had lunch instead. That was typical Harry. You went out to do one thing and ended up doing something entirely different.

On the way back to the theatre Harry stopped for petrol and another customer came over.

'I bet you get this all the time,' he said apologetically, 'but you don't half look like Harry Worth.'

Of course big mouth me couldn't resist saying, 'What are you talking about? It *is* Harry Worth,' and Harry found himself signing autographs right left and centre. I thought if that ever happens to me I'll know I've made it. It seemed the epitome of fame: the idea that your face is so well known it's instantly recognisable but people think you're too big a star ever to walk into their local petrol station.

The idea was reinforced a few weeks later when the same thing happened to Cary Grant. Cary Grant was in Bournemouth and he came to see the show. I didn't meet him myself, but Harry did and afterwards he told me that Cary's one wish was to go into a pub for a pint then go on for fish and chips. The people who were looking after him couldn't very well refuse but they'd warned him that he'd be driven mad by autograph hunters.

In fact all that happened was people kept saying, 'I bet you get this all the time, but you do look like Cary Grant.'

And Cary would agree that he did, and that was the end of the conversation.

There were quite a few shows in Bournemouth that summer and across the road from us was the play *Lock up your Daughters* featuring Anne Sydney, who had recently been Miss World.

At this time my press agent George Bartram was always thinking up stunts for me, and one day he rang with his latest brainwave.

'Mike, I've had an idea,' he said in his strong Birmingham accent. 'You know Anne Sydney's appearing across the road?'

'Yes,' I said warily.

'Well, would you like to do some photographs with her?'

Now I was such a small name that I was ranked under the printer on the bill. 'George,' I said, 'she won't want to be photographed with me. She's probably never heard of me.'

'Oh no, she would,' said George. 'She's ever such a nice girl you know. I'll give her a ring and get her to pop over and see you because her show finishes before yours.'

I humoured George but I couldn't believe that an ex-Miss

World would want to be bothered with me and when I put the phone down I forgot about the conversation.

A couple of nights later the stage door man knocked at my dressing room door.

'There's a Miss Anne Sydney at the stage door to see you,' he said.

I thought it was a joke. 'Oh yeah, sure there is,' I said sarcastically.

'No, really. She *is*. She's standing at the door.'

I had a few minutes to spare before the finale so although I was convinced someone was having me on, I went out to the stage door. And there, tall and elegant, stood a beautiful girl – the ex-Miss World, Anne Sydney.

'Hello, Mike,' said Anne. 'George asked me to come over and talk to you about some photographs.'

I was still very young and the thought that this lovely girl had come over to see me was quite overwhelming. Somehow I managed to lead her to my dressing room, and as we walked through the backstage corridors George Bartram's words came back to me.

'Now whatever you do make sure you take her to dinner, and somewhere nice too.'

'Would you like to go out to dinner?' I asked nervously, half hoping she would say no.

'Oh yes, that would be lovely,' Anne replied.

'Well I've just got to do the finale; I won't be long,' I said and rushed out, leaving her watching the portable television in my dressing room.

But when I came off stage I didn't go straight back to Anne. Instead I dived into Harry's dressing room where he and Joe Henderson were discussing the night's show.

'Oh Harry, I've got Miss World, Anne Sydney, in my room and I've got to take her out to dinner,' I gasped. 'Will you come with me?'

'You don't want me along with Miss World,' said Harry.

'Yes I do. And you, Joe. You come as well.'

'Come on, Mike. You don't want us!' they said.

'I *do*!' I insisted.

So Anne, Harry, Joe and I all set off to The Bistro. Harry and Joe drew the line at sharing a table with us, but they sat nearby for moral support. And in fact it was an enjoyable evening. I soon discovered that Anne Sydney was a very nice woman who just happened to have won a major beauty contest.

I saw quite a lot of Anne after that. She lived in Poole and took me over to her house once or twice and introduced me to the cast of *Lock up your Daughters*. We weren't in love with each other though and gradually the romance petered out. Then one evening I was talking to Craig Douglas who was in the play with Anne when I noticed a pretty blonde girl. I've always liked blondes.

'Who's that?' I asked Craig.

'That's Liz,' he said. 'I'll introduce you.'

Liz had a tiny part in the play but we'd not met before. I became very smitten with her and fell in love for the first time. I thought I'd been in love before but realised I couldn't have been because it wasn't like this.

We started going out and soon we were together all the time. After a while Liz moved into the flat I'd rented and everything was wonderful. We were together for almost the whole summer season – eighteen to twenty weeks – and we saw more of each other than most couples because we had every day free, apart from a couple of matinees, and we only worked for a few hours at night. It was a lovely summer, one of the most enjoyable periods of my life.

Then everything changed. The season finished, Liz had to go back to London and suddenly it was all over. I went to see her there but she wrote to me afterwards to say that our relationship was over. She even returned the watch I'd bought her.

It was a very painful experience. A love affair is wonderful when everything's going well, but when it ends it's like a bereavement. I managed to get Liz on the phone a few times after that but I couldn't get another date. It was heartbreaking.

I suppose everyone's been through a similar experience at some stage of their life. It certainly took me a long time to get over it: I carried a torch for Liz for the next two years. The only way to take my mind off her was to work, and I threw myself into my career as never before.

CHAPTER 6

Pantomimes and Practical Jokes

Ralph Reader's face was a picture. Dressed as the wicked Baron Fitzwarren in the pantomime *Dick Whittington*, he was supposed to plant a stolen ruby in Whittington's rucksack then 'discover' it later, proving that Whittington was the thief.

'Let me have a look at this rucksack,' demanded Ralph right on cue.

'All right,' said Joe Brown, who was playing Dick Whittington, handing it over.

And just as he'd done night after night, Ralph plunged in his hand, ready to deliver the next line: 'Look, he stole the ruby!' as he held the jewel aloft.

The line didn't come. There was a long pause as Ralph groped in the bag, his fingers scrabbling in increasing desperation to locate the ruby. He couldn't find it, which was hardly surprising since it wasn't there. Joe Brown had removed it earlier for a joke.

'The ruby is in here!' Ralph cried at last, flinging the rucksack away across the stage in digust.

And Joe and I could hardly get our lines out for laughing.

It was the Bachelors who introduced me to pantomime with

Puss in Boots in Bristol and from then on I acted in them regularly until 1971 when I decided that enough was enough.

I never really enjoyed them. I wasn't that sort of performer and when it got to the bit where you're supposed to do your own act, I knew I had a problem because the children wouldn't appreciate my topical jokes. In the end I got round it by doing impressions and getting the kids to guess the subject. They would make a hell of a lot of noise, which they enjoyed, then I would throw sweets to them, which they enjoyed even more, and everyone would be happy.

Despite appearances to the contrary pantomimes are hard work, and they can also be extremely boring for the performers. The only one I can truthfully say I enjoyed throughout was *Dick Whittington* at Golders Green. The lead role of Dick is a straight role but Joe Brown played it like a comic, just like Max Miller. And with Joe and Ralph Reader in the same show, you couldn't help but have a laugh.

I was playing Idle Jack and one day when things were starting to get dull Ralph said, 'Let's put a new gag in tonight, son' (he always called Joe and me son).

'All right,' I agreed.

'I'll come on,' he said, 'and I'll say to you: "Hey, what d'you know, Jack, I just got a television set for my mother in law' and you say: "Well that's a good swop." '

'OK, we'll give it a try.'

We put it in and the kids seemed to like it so we kept it in. It went well until one night towards the end of the run when Ralph was feeling tired.

'Hey, what d'you know Jack,' he said, 'I've just bought my mother in law a television set.'

'Well,' I replied, my voice trailing away, 'that's a good ... swop.'

We didn't get any laughs from the audience that night, just a puzzled silence. The cast enjoyed it, though.

I should think that everyone's missed a cue at some point in their career, but during *Dick Whittington* Ralph managed to do the opposite. He came on about a page and a half too soon and found himself on stage overhearing a scene that his character wasn't supposed to know about.

Ralph stared blankly at Joe. 'Sorry, son,' he said and turned round and walked off.

That was another puzzling moment for the audience.

As the last show approached everyone ad-libbed more and more outrageously. One night when it was mainly an adult audience I decided to liven up Idle Jack's poignant scene with the girl he loved.

'Mary, I do love you,' he said to his sweetheart, but she was in love with Whittington.

'I'm sorry, Jack, you're very sweet,' she replies, 'but I love Dick.'

'I know you do,' I snapped, not a bit like Idle Jack, 'that's how you got the part, isn't it, you silly cow?' and I walked off.

The band were on the floor laughing. It was very naughty of course, but that's the sort of thing you did to relieve the monotony.

I was in another pantomime where the villain was played by a serious straight actor. As usual the cast stuck to the script at the beginning but towards the end we started ad-libbing. One night I walked in and the villain said as usual,

'Ah, there you are.'

And for some reason I replied, 'Jessie Matthews.'

Quick as a flash the villain capped me with, 'I'll throw you over my shoulder' (Jessie Matthews' famous song being 'Over My Shoulder').

After that every time I said something, he capped it.

'There aren't any straight men left,' I complained jokingly one evening.

'Well there's you,' he said.

Half the time he didn't realise what he said until the words were out and after that little episode I think he feared he'd offended me.

'I'm awfully sorry,' he said as we walked off stage, 'I'll stop doing it.'

'No,' I said, 'it's wonderful; keep it in and surprise me every night.'

Unfortunately performers in a show don't always get on so well together. From the point of view of harmony backstage it's not a good idea to have too many struggling young comics on the same bill for instance, because each one jostles to become the comedy hit of the show.

There can also be arguments over who does which joke because several comics might include the same topical subject in their act. The scripts are different but the subject's the same, and such repetition has to be avoided in the interests of a varied show. The question is, who drops the gag from his act?

Arguments backstage are one thing, but worst of all are the arguments that spill over on to the stage itself. One night comedian Freddie Davis and I had a row. We were both part of the Bachelors' team at the time and both struggling for success, which didn't help. Anyway, a row blew up over something silly. I think Freddie wanted me to give a lift to someone and I didn't want to do it. There were sharp words after which we didn't speak to each other for three weeks.

It was all very well backstage – we could avoid each other – but we were appearing in *Puss in Boots* at the time and during the pantomime we had to appear in scenes together and speak dialogue to each other. It was horrible, not talking to someone yet having to talk to them.

We buried the hatchet in the end of course and got on well after that. Freddie was a great practical joker. We often shared a room when we were touring and I never knew what would happen next. One night after the show we were relaxing in the bar at our hotel.

'I'm tired,' said Freddie after a while; 'I think I'll go up to bed now.'

OK,' I said, 'I'll stay a bit longer.'

It must have been nearly an hour later when I followed Freddie upstairs and I expected to find him sound asleep. Instead the room was empty. The bed was untouched and there was no sign of him. He must have gone out, I thought to myself. I took off my jacket, went to the cupboard to hang it up and as my hand touched the knob, the door flew open and Freddie leapt out at me. I nearly had a heart attack, it was so unexpected.

Thinking about it afterwards what impressed me most was the planning: Freddie must have waited patiently for an hour to do that joke. In his place I think I would have given up and gone to bed long before.

Performers are notorious practical jokers and I was just as bad myself. I remember once I was appearing at the Theatre Club in Wakefield when a producer called David O'Clee who I'd known for some time came up to see me. He had a great sense of humour and when the manager walked into the dressing room where we were talking, he joined me in a quite spontaneous joke.

'Hello, Martin,' I said to the manager, 'what time will I be on?'

'About eleven o'clock,' he replied.

'I'd better get moving then,' I said and for some reason, I don't know why, I turned to David and said, 'Do you mind if I ask you who you are because you've been sitting there for the last half-hour.'

David played along beautifully. Normally he had a very correct BBC voice but instantly he went into this shifty character with a strange nasal twang.

'My name is Roy Bender,' he said, 'and I was wondering if I could have an autograph.'

'Certainly,' I said. I reached out for a photograph and started to sign my name. As I wrote, Martin Dale, the manager, glared at 'Roy Bender', because he was very strict about members of the public coming backstage. I handed the autographed picture to David, who examined it at great length.

'Can you sign it to Margery?' he asked.

I took it back and added the words "To Margery".

David peered at my writing once more.

'Oh, and could you put "To Audrey with love"?'

I did as he asked.

'OK,' I said, handing the photograph back for the last time, 'would you mind leaving now because I really must get ready to go on stage.'

David rose, but before he could take a step Martin Dale blocked his path.

'How the hell did you get in here?'

'Oh,' he said, 'I just walked in.'

'Well, you can just bloody well walk out,' said Martin angrily. Now Martin is a big man and he picked David up by the lapels, carried him out of my dressing room, walked the length of the corridor, opening three swing doors with him, and finally deposited him in the car park.

As they disappeared I could hear David insisting in his normal voice, 'I really am from the BBC you know,' but Martin paid no attention.

It was a very funny sight but the joke backfired because Martin was really angry.

'He *was* from the BBC, you know,' I told Martin when he returned.

Martin was furious.

'I've just fired both my bouncers and the receptionist,' he shouted.

They were all reinstated of course, but the episode taught me to be a little more careful with my jokes in future.

All this time I was steadily improving my act. No matter where I was I found time to watch television and new characters came and went from my repertoire. Harold Wilson had won the two previous elections and was well established as prime minister now so there was no need to continue with Macmillan. Malcolm Muggeridge and the Steptoes were still popular, and I'd added Ken Dodd since Liverpool, but it was important to be topical.

One evening I realised that Frankie Howerd, who had been a big name a few years before then faded a bit, was back. He appeared at the Establishment Club and tore the place up. From then on he went from strength to strength. There was no doubt about it, I had to put him in the act. I worked very hard at Frankie and often ended up with a sore throat. I realise now that I was straining unnecessarily but at the time it seemed the only way.

Then, as now, people used to say, 'You must spend hours practising your characters,' but I didn't really. I had a go in private and then when I was reasonably satisfied I put them into the act and let them develop naturally.

In those days of course I didn't have a video recorder to help me. I checked facial expressions in the mirror and worked on the voice by playing it over and over again in my head. I've always been able to think of a voice and then hear it in my mind. Most people can, I think.

But there was no better way of developing a character than by performing it every night, and in those days there was always somewhere to perform. My first attempts were often quite poor: my early Harold Wilson for instance was nowhere near as good as the later one; but you improve as you go along.

Quite a lot of my material was 'written' on stage. I went on with a sketchy outline of what I wanted to say then let the character take over. That was how catchphrases like Harold Wilson's 'And I said this at the Brighton conference ...' were born.

Years later Harold Wilson said to me, 'I didn't say that, you know.'

'Of course you didn't,' I replied. 'I made it up.'

'No,' he said, 'it was Blackpool!'

In character I was never stuck for something to say and it was always appropriate to that particular character. Sometimes this got me into trouble. Years later I was doing Bob Monkhouse and he was telling a joke about the smallest books in the world.

'*The Book of Famous Jewish Cricketers, The Book of Italian War Heroes* and *The Wit of Max Bygraves*,' said Bob.

Afterwards Max tackled me.

'What about this gag you're doing, the smallest book in the world, *The Wit of Max Bygraves*?'

'Oh,' I said, 'I was doing Bob Monkhouse.'

'What's that got to do with it?' asked Max.

I was genuinely surprised. 'Well it wasn't me. It was Bob. I wouldn't have done it, it's not my type of gag, but it's the type of gag Bob Monkhouse would do.'

'That's the best get-out I've ever heard,' said Max. 'So what d'you want me to do now? Ring Bob Monkhouse up and tackle him about it?'

Now Max is an old friend and I didn't want to offend him, but I seriously felt that I wasn't responsible.

I've known Max Bygraves a long time and he's the only performer who's ever given me advice. In 1967 when I was appearing with the Bachelors at Manchester Opera House, Max took over for a week while the boys went to a song festival. He was the star of the show in the star dressing room and I was in a little cubbyhole up four flights of stairs. Yet one night he climbed all those stairs to come and talk to me. He'd watched my act and gave me a lot of hints on improving my presentation. He suggested when I should slow things down, when I should speed them up and he even explained how I should wear my jacket.

'Mike, you're wearing a two-piece suit and leaving the jacket undone,' he said. 'It looks terrible. Only undo the jacket if you're wearing a waistcoat. A two-piece suit should always be buttoned.'

Travelling round the country as I did I came across quite a few speciality acts. These were the acts that opened the show, the jugglers, acrobats and knife-throwers. A lot of them were circus people and they came with their families in caravans and lived in the car park all week.

Some of them had animal acts. I remember one couple who toured with twelve performing poodles and another who used dozens of doves, one of which once escaped into the auditorium and flew around the audience for the rest of the show.

In one place my dressing room adjoined that of the speciality act which I hadn't seen. I was always getting ready while he was on stage. What puzzled me though was that every night when he came off I heard him being sick in his room. I couldn't understand it. It's quite common for nervous performers to throw up before the show, but not afterwards.

After listening to his suffering for several nights in a row I was so intrigued that the following evening I made a point of getting ready early so that I could watch him work.

It turned out he was a fire-eater.

'That's terrible,' I said to him once he'd composed himself after finishing his act.

'Yes I know,' he said. 'And I have to do this every night when I come off.'

Apparently fire-eating left him with a throat full of burnt paper and the only way he could get the paper out was to throw up. It seemed a dreadful way to make a living.

Fortunately I didn't have such problems. The topical subjects I chose seemed to be appreciated by the audiences and I got some wonderful reviews. Yet I can't claim to have gone down well everywhere. At around this time I had my worst booking in twenty-five years of show business.

This was when I died a terrible death at a private function at the Adelphi Hotel in Liverpool. It was a twenty-five years' service celebration. There had been a dinner, lots of people had been presented with clocks then I came on to do the cabaret.

'When are you going to get the right time?' I asked jokingly.

All right, perhaps it's not such a funny gag, but it was met by total silence. Not a flicker. I ploughed on, doing impressions that had raised big laughs the night before. But there was nothing. No response at all. It was almost frightening. I walked off to polite though restrained applause, feeling as if I'd been put through a mangle.

What really twisted my mind though was a remark I heard as I was leaving.

'It's been a lovely evening,' said one man to his wife.

'Yes, I've enjoyed it as well,' she replied as she buttoned her coat. 'Pity about the cabaret though, wasn't it?'

Although I know you can't expect to please everyone, I still felt deeply hurt.

Most of the time, thank goodness, the reaction was just the opposite, and in 1967 things were going so well for me that the BBC decided to put me in a series with Lulu and Ray Fell. Called *Three of a Kind*, it was to be screened on BBC 2. It was a very good opportunity for me because it gave me the chance to build up television experience without the pressure of carrying the whole show myself. My Palladium appearances and Ray's camera-training stood me in good stead, and I didn't find it difficult to adapt.

Unfortunately I didn't ever see the series because I was doing a summer season in Great Yarmouth when it was screened, and at the time you couldn't get BBC 2 in Great Yarmouth. My mother and father enjoyed it, of course, and were full of praise, but if some of the old clips I've seen recently are anything to go by, I expect I was very raw.

It was in Great Yarmouth that I had my only real brush with death, as opposed to 'dying a death'. I'd rented a house for the season and this particular night I invited a lot of people back for drinks after the show. The party went on until the early hours then everyone started to drift away. Practically everyone had gone and I was left with a girl I fancied.

'Would you like to stay?' I asked.

'No,' she said firmly, 'I've got to go home now.'

'It's all right,' I said, 'I've got three bedrooms in this house; you'll be OK.'

But she wanted to be taken home, so despite the fact that I'd had quite a lot to drink and she lived about ten miles away, I got out the car. I was driving a Daimler Sovereign by this time – I was at the stage when I wanted the nicest car I could afford.

Anyway, we set off down these dark, windy lanes, and everything was fine until in the middle of nowhere a car came straight towards us without dipping its headlights. I was completely blinded. The car swept on and too late I saw a tight bend rushing towards us. I started to turn the wheel but there wasn't time. The Daimler went straight on into woodland, crashing and lurching over bushes and uneven ground, the headlights picking out undergrowth and trees.

It seemed to go on for ever. My only thought was that I wanted the car to stop. At last there was a great bang as we hit a fallen tree, and we came to a halt.

The girl and I looked at each other. This was before the days of compulsory seat belts and we weren't wearing them, but we'd been incredibly lucky. I'd hit my head on the roof of the car and she'd banged her forehead on the screen. That was all. We were both more or less unhurt and when we realised this, we burst out laughing. It was shock of course, but we climbed out to inspect the damage laughing hysterically. Even the sight of my beautiful Daimler with the front smashed in didn't bring me to my senses. If I hadn't been driving such a big, solid car I think we would have been killed.

We walked back to the road, where a taxi returning late to Great Yarmouth spotted us, stopped and took us to the local hospital for a check-up.

Fortunately neither of us suffered any ill effects from the accident but the Daimler was a write-off.

My driving was never the same again. Until then I'd always driven rather fast. From that moment on I became a much more cautious driver and to this day I'm not a great lover of speed.

CHAPTER 7

Wedding Bells

I noticed the girl as soon as she walked into the rehearsal room. She was small and blonde and was holding a white poodle on a lead. There was something about her that reminded me of Liz, though if you'd stood them side by side an impartial observer would probably have noticed no resemblance whatsoever.

'Who's that?' I asked Johnny Greenland, the choreographer.

Johnny was a wonderful character; outrageously camp. He used to come into rehearsal and say things like, 'Sorry I'm late. It's jelly week at Sainsburys.' For once though, he was serious.

'Oh, that's Sandra,' he said. 'She's a very nice girl, but be nice to her. She's lost her fiancé. He was killed in a road accident.'

I glanced across at Sandra again and as I did so the thought suddenly flashed through my mind, 'She's the one for me.'

1968 turned out to be one of my best years ever, after a slightly shaky start. I was still very young and my ego was growing faster than my success. I didn't realise it at the time but I was becoming a bighead. I was terrible.

Three of a Kind went down well and we did a second series, but by then I was getting unbearable. A third series was planned. Now this would have been good news but for the fact that this was to go ahead without Lulu because she was getting her own show. I was jealous. I wanted my own show and in a fit of pique because I wasn't offered one, I turned down the new series. I was in no position to refuse anything at that stage of the game, as my agent tried to warn me, but I wouldn't listen. I was too bigheaded to believe him.

I was lucky my television career didn't end there and then. As it was, Lew Grade saved things for me. He was putting on a Royal Gala at the Palladium to help finance the British Olympic team, and he invited me to appear. The Queen was to be present and so was Harold Wilson, the Prime Minister, who was also featuring as the climax to my act at that time.

'What are you going to do in the Harold Wilson part?' asked Lew Grade.

'Oh, I've got a script,' I said vaguely.

Lew shook his head. 'Be careful. We don't want anything political with the Queen here. Just come on and say good evening or whatever and leave it at that.'

I was in despair. Harold Wilson was the most popular part of my act. I felt sure it would fall flat if I left him out, but what was the point of coming on with the pipe and mac and saying 'Good evening'? That would hardly leave them rolling in the aisles.

I had a moan about it to Jimmy Tarbuck who was also in the show.

'Why don't you come on, look down at Wilson and say "Snap"?' said Jimmy.

I thought about it. It might work. 'Thanks, Jimmy. I'll give it a try,' I said.

On the night, despite my usual nerves, I enjoyed myself. The audience was great. They laughed at everything and when, at the end of my spot, I put on the Gannex raincoat and picked up the pipe, there was an extra little ripple of anticipation because they knew Harold Wilson was present. I walked down to the front of the stage, opened my mouth as if to begin the Harold Wilson dialogue then I stopped short and pretended to do a double take at the sight of the Prime Minister and his wife, as if I'd noticed them for the first time.

I stared at Harold Wilson, with my Harold Wilson face. There was a long pause, then, with my Harold Wilson voice, I said, 'And as for you, sir, I've got only one thing to say to you – snap!' then I hurried off stage as if I'd lost my nerve at the sight of him and dared not say more.

There was a great roar of appreciation from the house and I think the improvised climax went down even better than the original would have done.

After the show we all lined up in the foyer to meet the Queen. I'd always thought that on occasions like that you were briefed on what to say and do. Well, you're not. We were simply requested not to squeeze the Queen's hand tightly.

'Just extend your right hand,' I was told, 'and the Queen will shake it.'

After that, as the Queen advanced down the line of people towards me all I could think was 'don't squeeze her hand, don't squeeze her hand'.

'What was she wearing?' my mother asked later on the phone.

I couldn't remember. I hadn't noticed. I had a confused impression of a tiara, lots of jewels and long gloves. I distinctly remember the gloves as I concentrated on not squeezing her hand.

She was surprisingly small and, like other royal ladies, as I was to discover later, she didn't seem to wear perfume. There was no scent from her at all. You couldn't smell make-up or hairspray or any perfume whatsoever.

'Most enjoyable,' said the Queen, shaking my limp fingers. 'Have you been doing this long?'

I told her how long I'd been in show business.

'It must be marvellous to be other people,' she remarked as she passed on.

Then pausing, as if she'd remembered something, she turned back.

'Oh, by the way,' she added, 'don't worry. The Prime Minister was laughing!'

I got some marvellous reviews for the Gala and as a result Lew Grade signed me up for my own show with ATV. The contract was for three shows but if they went well, Dave Forrester told me, the contract was likely to be renewed.

It was a busy time. The series coincided with a season at the Palladium where I was appearing with Cliff Richard, so I was rehearsing for ATV during the day then doing the show at night. Yet I still found time to fall in love.

Instinctively I had known the first time I had seen Sandra Burville that she was the one for me. Doing something about it was another matter. Sandra was a dancer and she always seemed to be with the other girls. What's more, I was too shy to speak to her and she was too shy to speak to me.

In the end it was Dilys Watling who brought us together. Dilys did some comedy routines in the show and after a few days in rehearsal watching me watching Sandra, she realised how I felt. I confessed to her that I was attracted to Sandra. Not long afterwards, and unknown to me, Sandra told Dilys how much she liked me.

The next thing I knew Dilys was having a dinner party and I was invited. I arrived to find Lionel Blair, his girlfriend Sue and Sandra sipping drinks before dinner. It was a lovely surprise and a great evening. We all knew each other, my shyness disappeared and soon Sandra and I were getting on fine together.

I'd come in a cab so Sandra ran me back to my hotel and we started going out together from then on. While I was appearing at the Palladium, Sandra was dancing in a musical called *Lady be Good* at the Saville Theatre not far away, and we used to meet up afterwards. One of our favourite places was the Lotus House restaurant in Edgware Road, and Sandra used to laugh about our first meal there.

I wasn't a big eater at the time and I wasn't particularly keen on Chinese food, so that night I sat there picking at my meal and very soon I was finished. I stopped eating and almost at once Sandra stopped eating too.

Years later she told me, 'I wanted to make a good impression so you wouldn't think I was greedy. So when you stopped eating I stopped, but I was *starving*!'

After all that dancing she probably went home and made herself a sandwich!

Often we were too tired to go out and Sandra would go back to her flat, I'd go back to my hotel and we'd talk for ages on the phone. We both had very tiring schedules. As well as rehearsals all day and our respective shows at night, there were two shows on Saturday then a trip to Birmingham on Sunday to record the TV series.

I could have done without the Palladium booking at that particular moment, but naturally it was good experience. I marvelled at the tact of Cliff's manager, Peter Gormley. In those days I couldn't tell the difference between good and bad taste and one of my remarks obviously struck Cliff as a bit tacky.

After my act I introduced Cliff and all the girls screamed. 'All right, all right,' I tutted one evening in Frankie Howerd's voice, 'don't get your knickers in a twist.'

It got a big laugh so after that I put it in regularly.

'Mike,' said Peter Gormley a few nights later when I came

off stage, 'you know that "knickers in a twist" line you do before Cliff comes on?'

'The Frankie Howerd bit?'

'Yes.' He looked embarrassed. 'Look, don't tell Cliff I mentioned it, because he'd go mad if he knew I'd said anything, but could you take it out?'

I was surprised. 'Sure,' I said, 'but what's the problem?'

'Well ... knickers ... you know ...' he pulled a face – 'but don't tell Cliff I mentioned it. He would hate to think I'd said anything.'

I took the line out immediately of course and I was impressed. Cliff obviously thought the joke was a bit down-market and wanted it out, but Peter Gormley had made sure there would be no unpleasantness between Cliff and me by taking the responsibility on himself. In fact of course there wouldn't have been any unpleasantness, but Peter wasn't taking any chances. That's what you call good management.

Not long afterwards I narrowly escaped offending Cliff again with another sample of bad taste. Every Saturday there was a dull, hanging around spell between the matinee and the evening performance, and this particular afternoon one of the comedians in the show came into my dressing room with a friend.

'Mike, you've got a bit of time, haven't you?'

I nodded.

'I've got a blue movie in the car. We could show it on your door. What d'you think?'

The door of my dressing room happened to be cream, an ideal background for showing a movie, and I was very bored.

'OK, bring it in,' I said.

A few minutes later we were sitting watching the movie when the door opened and Cliff stood there. He was wearing a white shirt and white trousers which provided an even better background for the movie than the door.

'Oh sorry,' he said, 'I didn't know you were showing a film.'

'It's all right,' I said, hypnotised by the sight of naked women rippling across Cliff's shirt, 'er ... this fella's been to Australia and he's boring us with his holiday movie.'

'Oh – well I just wanted to know when Terry's coming?'

Terry was the hairdresser we shared while we were at the Palladium.

'About half an hour, I think.'

'All right, give me a shout when he gets here, could you? Sorry to disturb your film.'

And he went away, never knowing that he'd taken part in the screening of a blue movie.

Around this time Sandra was excited because the dancers from *Lady be Good* had been invited to take part in that year's Royal Variety Performance. The Palladium was to be taken over one Sunday in November for the show and all the top stars were appearing. I hadn't been invited and I hadn't expected to be, but I was very pleased for Sandra. Having met the Queen at the Royal Gala earlier in the year, I knew what a great thrill it would be.

Then came the sad news that Eric Morecambe had suffered a heart attack and therefore Morecambe and Wise, who should have been the stars of the show, would have to pull out.

It didn't occur to me that I might be a replacement. As far as I was concerned I'd had my turn at the Royal Gala. I was genuinely sorry to hear about Eric and I was only glad that he seemed to be recovering well.

Then one day Dave phoned me urgently. I was wanted for the variety performance after all. Morecambe and Wise had been down for two spots, so could I fill one, while Frankie Howerd filled the other?

There was really no need to ask. It seemed an incredible stroke of luck that Sandra and I should both appear in the same Royal Variety Show. Even more thrilling was the discovery that I would be sharing the number one dressing room. I already had my own dressing room at the Palladium for the weekday show with Cliff, but Eric and Ernie had been alloted the number one dressing room so now it belonged to Frankie Howerd and me. I was duly moved out of my modest little room and into the star quarters. In fact the star dressing room was much the same as the others, only bigger, but I was delighted to be there nevertheless.

The only thing that slightly marred the evening was Frankie's disapproval of my impression of him. Strangely enough in all these years he's the only person who's ever admitted to my face that he didn't care for being mimicked.

'You make me look effeminate,' he said.

I didn't know what to say to that. I'd never considered Frankie Howerd to be an effeminate comic. His way of telling a story comes across to me as a woman's way of talking over the garden wall, rather than a homosexual's way of speaking.

'This bird came over to me,' I used to say in Frank's voice, 'and I fancied her. Yeerrs, and I think she fancied me, but when we got back to her place she turned out to be a bit kinky. She said, "Let's make love like cats." And we tried it and fell off the bloody roof ...' Well, I couldn't see that there was anything homosexual about that.

'I'm sorry if that's the impression you get, Frank,' I said, 'but it's not intentional. That's not the way I see you at all.'

After the show we lined up as before to shake hands with the Royal Family. The Queen wasn't present this time, instead there was the Queen Mother, Prince Charles, Princess Anne and Princess Margaret. They were all lovely and I noticed that the Queen Mother in particular was much more forthright than the Queen. The Queen had been polite but noncommittal as she passed down the line, whereas her mother was more positive.

'That's a very pretty dress you're wearing,' I heard her say to someone further along.

'I can't understand how you actually *become* Harold Wilson,' she said when she got to me. 'It's almost frightening.'

I didn't know quite what to make of that.

Later Sandra and I went out to celebrate a memorable evening with a meal at the Lotus House.

Yes, 1968 was a wonderful year. I rounded it off by taking Sandra home at Christmas to meet my mother. Mum was a bit reserved at first. She tended to think that every girl was after my money or something, but in the end Sandra's lovely personality won her round and my mother adored her from then on.

Like 1968, 1969 didn't start well but it improved steadily. Early in the year came my biggest disappointment since I had failed to become compere of the Cabaret Club. Despite a good reception for my three television shows, Lew Grade didn't renew my contract. I was bitterly disappointed.

'*Why* aren't they renewing it?' I asked Dave when he broke the news to me.

'You're a bit too big-headed,' said Dave bluntly.

I was amazed. I wasn't aware of it at all, but looking back I suppose it couldn't be helped. I hadn't been around very long, a lot of exciting things had happened and it does affect you, especially when you're young.

Depression set in for a week or two. I was convinced the bubble had burst and that I was on the way down. Nevertheless Dave continued to get me a lot of work. The clubs were still going strong and I was booked for the summer season in Bournemouth with Fankie Vaughan. I wasn't exactly sitting at home waiting for the phone to ring.

Best of all, I was in love. My relationship with Sandra had blossomed into something special and finally I found the courage to propose. Well almost. Whenever I'm nervous or embarrassed I tend to say things in other voices and faced with asking Sandra to marry me I went into just about every other character but my own.

'Mike,' said Sandra at last, 'if you've got something to say to me, say it yourself.'

So I asked her to marry me and to my surprise she said yes.

I was in the middle of a summer season at the time and everyone at the theatre was full of congratulations. Frankie Vaughan, a warm, affectionate man, was particularly delighted. So much so that he couldn't resist announcing the engagement from the stage.

Frank has a relaxed, chatty style with an audience. He talks to them as if they were personal friends and tells them about people he likes. If someone in the band is celebrating a birthday he mentions it, and so it was quite natural to him to want to share our good news.

'Ladies and gentlemen,' he said, 'in the audience tonight we've got Mike Yarwood's fiancée. They're getting married in November and we wish them well. I would like to dedicate my next song to Sandra. Sandra, where are you sitting?'

To Sandra's horror, the spotlights swung about the audience until they found her then Frank insisted that she left her seat and came down to the front of the stage by the orchestra pit, where he sang a song to her. It was a nice thought but Sandra said afterwards that she was very embarrassed. Odd really, considering she was in show business herself.

Frankie Vaughan was another personality who went into my act after a shared booking. He's a great performer. I loved to watch him strutting the stage – he did it so beautifully that I wanted to do it too. I was intrigued to learn that he brushed his top hat to make it shine and that it was the same hat he'd used for years. If you looked at it closely you could see that it was a little frayed at the edges but Frank wouldn't part with it. I believe he's still using his original cane too.

From Frank I learned that if you want to be a star you have to be a star all the time, not just on the stage. It was a lesson I didn't put into practice myself unfortunately, and a few years later Danny La Rue gave me a real ticking off about it. We were attending a function in Blackpool together and I arrived unshaven. Danny was furious.

'You should always be a star,' he said. 'You should look like one when you walk into any room, not just when you walk on stage.'

Frankie Vaughan understood this instinctively. At any time of the day or night, no matter where he was or what he was doing, he always looked like a star.

This was a very happy time in my life. Sandra and I were madly in love and spent all our free time house-hunting. Although I travelled a great deal, staying in hotels around the country, I still officially lived at home with my parents in Bredbury and I wanted to stay in Cheshire after the wedding. Sandra didn't mind. Originally from Brighton, she had already uprooted once when she came to London to work as a dancer and she had no special feelings for the capital. We wanted to start a family right away, so we were searching for a quiet place to bring up children.

We were much more fortunate than most young couples our age because we didn't have to worry much about money. We could afford to pay up to £12,000, and in those days you could get a nice house for that much. Yet we looked all over the place and couldn't find anything we wanted.

'Why don't you look out Prestbury way?' said my mother one evening. 'It's a very nice area.'

So we did and she was right. Prestbury, near Macclesfield, was quiet and green and easy to reach. Just outside the village we found a seventeenth-century cottage called Old Dunbar for sale. It was beautiful: black and white outside, oak beams and inglenook fireplaces inside, with a big garden and surrounded by open fields. The only problem was the price: £18,000. But we'd fallen in love with it and had to have it.

My extravagance was really beginning to develop now. 'Don't worry,' I told Sandra, 'we can afford it,' and I arranged a mortgage which was almost double the amount we'd originally had in mind. But Old Dunbar was worth it. I didn't ever want to leave.

Our wedding was arranged for 8th November at the church of St Thomas More at Swiss Cottage in London, with a reception afterwards at the Royal Lancaster Hotel. My old friend David was to be best man, and the only worry was my mother. We would have been very sad if she hadn't come, but until the moment she arrived I wasn't sure if she would make it to the ceremony.

Over the years her illness had become gradually worse. Being away so often I suppose I didn't notice it as much as my father and Josephine, but even so I couldn't help realising there was something wrong. Some days I would arrive to find my mother lying on the settee in a state of fear and panic about nothing. Other days she was her normal self except for the fact that she hardly ever left the house.

Some people told her to snap out of it. Others said only you can help yourself. I tended to sympathise and I tried to make her laugh. I used to go into a funny character, no one in particular, and send up all the unwanted advice she was given.

'It's only you can help yourself, love ...' I'd say, my arms folded across my chest. 'You can snap out of it if you want to.'

And even when she was feeling rough I could make her laugh. Surely, I reasoned, it was better for her to laugh than to be tense. Josephine with her nursing experience tended to be tougher with Mum than I was, yet neither approach really seemed to help. Even the doctor couldn't seem to make any headway beyond prescribing valium.

I know Mum and Dad would have loved to come to the

Royal Variety Performance but my mother couldn't manage. How she got to our wedding I'll never know.

I didn't have a stag-night. The night before the wedding David and I went to confession at a Catholic church in Westminster. It was the first time I'd been in a church for years and to this day I can smell the incense and the candles of that night. Strangely enough there wasn't as much to own up to as I'd feared, and I felt much better for going.

The next morning I was so nervous I was physically sick, but the arrival of my parents helped take my mind off it. I was staying at the Royal Lancaster Hotel, which was a high rise building, and I could see straight away that my mother was a bit shaky.

'I can't look out of the windows,' she said, her lips white under her make-up.

So I went into my funny northern character, voicing her fears and turning them into jokes, and kept her laughing all the way to the church.

'These floors are no thicker than cardboard, you know; you can feel them shake,' I tutted as we went down in the lift, 'and the whole building blows in the wind ... it really sways. Fire trap of course, absolute fire trap ...'

We were in hysterics by the time we got to the church.

There was no time for a honeymoon after the wedding because I was booked for several weeks' cabaret at the Savoy Hotel, but that didn't seem to matter. As soon as the engagement ended we hurried off to Old Dunbar which seemed the nicest honeymoon spot we could have chosen.

CHAPTER 8

'Look — Mike Yarwood'

'There's a phone call for you, Mike.'

It was half-way through the show. I was working again with Frankie Vaughan, doing the Christmas season at the Royal Court Theatre, Liverpool, and phone calls at such a time were highly unusual.

Vaguely anxious, I hurried to the stage-door phone.

'Hello, darling, it's me,' said Sandra. 'I won't keep you. I just wanted you to know that it's official. I've heard from the doctor today.'

She was pregnant! When I had left Prestbury a few days before Sandra had been hopeful but not certain, and we'd both been keeping our fingers crossed ever since. Now the good news had come though.

I was thrilled. When I'd finished talking to Sandra and insisting that she rest, I ran into Frank's dressing room shouting, 'I'm going to be a father!' Frank, who's a great family man, was very pleased for us of course and after the show he took me out for a meal to celebrate.

The baby was due in September and I was booked for the summer season in Blackpool. There was a chance that the show

103

might finish three weeks early, and Sandra and I were both desperately hoping that this would happen. I wanted to stay at home and help with the baby.

At this time my personal life was much more satisfying than my career. Although I had plenty of work and was frequently asked to do guest appearances, I felt as if I wasn't getting anywhere professionally. I was still suffering the depressing sensation that the bubble had burst. Yet my ego trip continued. I'd become a professional snob: for example, I didn't like the fact that my Blackpool summer season was at the Queens Theatre, because the Queens wasn't the number one theatre in Blackpool. Neither did I like the fact that I wasn't even second top of the bill. I was third top of the bill. I had a row about that even though the other two stars were Winifred Attwell and Donald Peers.

Looking back I realise that Dave Forrester was very good. He didn't want to push me too far too fast, but made sure I established myself gradually.

'You're not ready for top of the bill yet,' he told me when I became impatient. 'Give it time.'

And of course he was absolutely right. Unlike some agents who work their clients almost to death as soon as they start to become popular, Dave believed that lasting success had to be built on solid foundations.

That summer of 1970 was the turning point. Despite the fact that I didn't like appearing at the Queens Theatre, it was there that my luck changed. One night I came off stage to find Bill Cotton from the BBC waiting in my dressing room.

'We'd like you to do a series, Mike,' he said after the polite preliminaries. Then, seeing my face, he added, 'Yes, it's going to be your show, although you'll have someone with you.'

The show was called *Look – Mike Yarwood*, and I worked with Adrienne Posta and Peter Noon. At last I was able to introduce some innovations, like the ventriloquist scene with

Robin Day as the ventriloquist working two dummies, one of Harold Wilson and one of Ted Heath. It was a very popular idea and the show marked the start of a long association with the BBC. I did a series a year for them for the next twelve years.

September arrived and the summer season dragged on. Sandra was growing larger by the day and I'd booked a room for her in St Mary's Hospital, Manchester at £150 a day. Extravagance again, I suppose, but if I could afford it I wanted her to have it.

On 19th September came the news that the labour had started and Sandra had gone to the hospital, but I was trapped at the theatre with a show to do. Throughout the evening while I was on stage I got a friend to phone the hospital every ten minutes.

Then as I came off after the finale he said, 'Congratulations, you've got a daughter.'

It was marvellous. Charlotte's birth gave me the greatest joy of my life. Nothing else compared with it and that includes getting my big Hercules bike when I was 13 and my first appearance on *Sunday Night at the London Palladium*.

We dashed into the theatre bar to wet the baby's head, and then I raced to the hospital. I was there by midnight – an hour and fifteen minutes after coming off stage, and Sandra had just woken up.

'Come on, I'll take you to see your daughter,' said the nurse. And she led us down the corridor to a room where seven babies lay sleeping in a row of cots.

The nurse wasn't sure which baby belonged to us. She walked down the line looking at the notes on each cot. Suddenly, as she paused beside the middle cot, I said, 'That's the one.'

She bent to examine the notes. 'Why yes,' she said in surprise, 'you're right, Mr Yarwood.'

'You were guessing,' said Sandra.

'No I wasn't. I knew,' I insisted, and to this day I'll swear I instinctively knew our baby.

She was beautiful: 7lb 3oz with dark hair and dark eyes, and perfect in every way.

'What d'you think about the name Charlotte?' asked Sandra, because we'd superstitiously not chosen one before the birth.

'Lovely,' I said.

A few days later when we brought her home from hospital and put her to bed I went up to peep in the cot and found myself weeping. I'd never cried with happiness before, but now I wept and wept. I felt such joy. She was so beautiful.

I soon learned how to hold a baby. Until then I'd been afraid to pick one up because I thought they were fragile, but Charlotte taught me how wrong I'd been. Babies are amazingly tough. One dreadful day when she was starting to crawl, Charlotte fell down the stairs. She rolled from top to bottom. We were frantic and rushed her round to the doctor's but there wasn't a bruise or a bump on her. Nevertheless it was a frightening experience.

With marriage and the family I became much more of a stay-at-home. Like the other young husbands in the area I still tended to go for a drink at six o'clock with the lads in the village pub, but I was always back by eight and then I loved to sit down with Sandra and relax. There was still a lot of work that took me away from home but when I wasn't working the only place I wanted to be was by the fire at Old Dunbar.

Charlotte grew stronger and more beautiful by the day and when she was a year old Sandra and I started talking about having another child. We both desperately wanted a boy and when Sandra discovered she was pregnant again, early in 1972, we kept our fingers crossed.

By this time the pattern of our marriage was well established. I was extravagant and Sandra was the thrifty one. She looked after the house, my office work and our financial affairs and she was very careful with money. She never seemed to spend anything on herself.

On the other hand I was always buying things. One night I was in the pub and I noticed the machine they'd bought for pressing oranges to make fresh orange juice.

'That's nice,' I said to Otto the barman. 'How much are they?'

'About £85,' he told me.

It didn't sound unreasonable. 'Could you get one for me?' I asked.

Otto thought he could and not long afterwards I became the proud owner of an £85 orange presser. True, it did make lovely orange juice – it crushed every bit of the fruit. The only problem was that it made gallons of juice at a time and someone had to stand there for about two hours loading oranges into it. It quickly ended up in the cupboard under the sink.

On another occasion I went to a charity auction and found myself bidding for an ancient Royal Variety programme. It had been specially made for King George VI and he'd left it behind on his seat in the Royal Box after the performance. It was printed on parchment and was rather special but I wasn't really bothered about having it until I realised that someone I didn't like was bidding against me. Immediately I was determined he shouldn't have it. The more he bid, the more I bid, until eventually we pushed the price up to £60 and he dropped out.

'Oh, this is nice,' said Sandra when I took it home later.

'Yes; it cost me £60.'

'Why?' asked Sandra, going off it rapidly.

'Well, I didn't like the chap who was bidding against me. I didn't want him to have it.'

Sandra didn't say anything but she must have thought I was crazy. Afterwards when she occasionally came across the programme in the back of a drawer she'd say, 'Oh, here's that programme you bought in the auction. That was money well spent, wasn't it, darling? We get a lot of use out of this!'

But Sandra let me have my own way. I liked nice things and I bought expensive furniture, beautiful rugs and, as soon as I could afford it, a Rolls Royce.

I also developed a compulsion for having more than one of everything. Perhaps there's a name for people like me.

'If you're going to the chemist's,' I would say to Sandra, 'I need a new toothbrush. Could you get me half a dozen?'

'Half a dozen?' Sandra would say. 'What d'you want half a dozen for?'

'Well, the way I brush my teeth they don't last long.' But that wasn't the real reason. In fact I'm not sure what the real reason was. Not greed. More a feeling that an object might get spoiled so I'd better have a spare. I could always rationalise it.

'I want a white silk jacket,' I told my tailor. 'Well actually I'm going to need two.'

He wasn't going to argue of course, but why two?

'Well, it's going to get grubby so I'll need two – one to wear while the other's in the cleaner's.' And these jackets cost £600 each! (I conveniently forgot that you can have a jacket cleaned in less than twenty-four hours).

When I needed a new dinner suit for summer season I bought six. My tailor told me that Tom Jones always ordered six at a time. Tom Jones of course was earning a lot more money than I was but that did it, I had to have six.

'It's because of wear and tear, you see, Sandra,' I'd explain. 'We do six shows a week, twice a night. I need a suit for every evening so that the creases fall out properly.'

Looking back it's frightening, and I still haven't got rid of the problem.

I would go out to buy a tie, see two I liked and end up buying four; two of each. So I would have four ties, two of which were identical. Why didn't I get four different colours or two different designs? Wear and tear again. They were silk ties you see, and silk ties tend to crinkle at the edges and look tired after a while ... and so on and so on.

Yet sometimes my extravagance was welcome. When Sandra was pregnant the second time I decided to buy her a mink coat. I went into a shop in Wilmslow in Cheshire and found an assistant who was about Sandra's size. She tried on the coat I'd chosen, a beautiful champagne mink, and she didn't want to take it off.

'I'll take it,' I said, 'but I would like it wrapped in some used brown paper, not a fancy box with your name on, and I would like it tied with string.'

There were some raised eyebrows in the shop but I was paying so they did as I asked.

Back home I walked in with the untidy parcel under my arm and dumped it on a chair.

'What's this?' asked Sandra, walking past it a few minutes later.

'Oh, I just went into a shop and bought a couple of raincoats,' I said. I got through a lot of raincoats playing Harold Wilson.

'Raincoats?' said Sandra. 'What d'you want more raincoats for? Let's have a look and see what you're wasting your money on now.'

She cut through the string with the kitchen scissors, folded back the brown paper then stopped in surprise. There was the mink coat, all satiny and beautiful.

'Oh Mike!' She lifted it clear of the paper and held it up to look at it and tears started to trickle down her cheeks.

'Don't you like it?' I asked.

'I love it!'

But my timing wasn't brilliant. When she tried on the coat Sandra couldn't fasten it because she was heavily pregnant at the time. It was like that joke about the girl who'll do anything for a mink coat and when she gets one she can't fasten it.

Our second child was born on 29th November, 1972 and to Sandra's disappointment, I wasn't there at the birth. To be honest I didn't really want to be. I was very old fashioned in those days and I thought that having babies was a woman's business. I also suspected that I'd be squeamish. Nevertheless for Sandra's sake I had agreed to be there and I braved myself to hold her hand throughout the whole thing.

As it turned out, I didn't have to. Sandra went into labour in the middle of the night. Charlotte was sound asleep, so we decided to leave her in her cot while I rushed Sandra to the hospital which was fourteen miles away. At the hospital I got her settled with the nurses then turned round and dashed home. I got Charlotte up and dressed and took her to a friend's house nearby, then I set off for the hospital once more. By now dawn had broken and on the outskirts of Manchester traffic was building. I was held up and by the time I got to the hospital it was all over.

We had another beautiful daughter. True, we were a little disappointed that she wasn't a boy, but we soon got over it. We were just grateful that she was a bright, healthy child.

The name was a problem. For some reason we'd both been convinced that the baby would be a boy and we'd only thought of boys' names. Clare came home from hospital without a name while we discussed the possibilities. I liked the name Joanna, but Sandra wasn't keen. In the end we were inspired by a pop song. Leo Sayer's hit record 'Clare' was number one in the charts around that time, and listening to it on the radio one day we were both struck by what a pretty name it was. I think a lot of other parents felt the same way because a great many of Clare's contemporaries are called the same thing.

Charlotte and Clare have grown into lovely children. Beautiful and blonde, they looked like a pair of little angels when they were young, and they were never any trouble. They didn't yell or screech or throw tantrums. Even as tiny babies they were good, and neither of them kept us up all night. They just woke for their feeds and went back to sleep again. We were very fortunate.

The arrival of a second baby meant another upheaval. Much as we loved Old Dunbar, we couldn't help realising that it was too small for our growing family. It had only two bedrooms and you had to walk through the main bedroom to reach the second, which wasn't a satsifactory layout with two children. Reluctantly we had to admit that it was time to move.

By now Sandra had made a lot of friends in the area and we didn't want to leave Prestbury, so we decided to wait until the right house came along. As it happened it came along quite quickly. Living on the spot we knew immediately when Prestbury House was put up for sale, and we were amongst the first people to look at it.

Much larger than Old Dunbar, it was an elegant Georgian-style building about forty years old. It had three floors, seven bedrooms and you could walk to the village through a little gate at the bottom of the garden. The one thing we couldn't complain of at Prestbury House was lack of space.

We bought it, moved in with the girls and set about making it into a home.

CHAPTER 9

Surviving the Seventies

Everything was happening for me. During the 1970s I had more success than I'd ever dreamed possible. My television shows had marvellous ratings, I did Christmas specials, summer seasons, winter seasons – I could have worked non-stop. I got good reviews, people recognised me wherever I went, I played in charity football matches with top football stars, I met politicans and royalty. It should have been wonderful.

Yet the 1970s were the unhappiest ten years of my life. I hated that decade.

It all started with a letter. I was appearing in a summer season in Scarborough at the time and was feeling lonely because Sandra and the children were away. Sandra had gone to visit her sister abroad and the girls were staying with their grandmother in Brighton because I couldn't look after them while I was working.

So there I was, sitting in my dressing room going through the mail. I wouldn't say I was snowed under with fan mail but I got my share. Anyway, half-way through the batch I unfolded a sheet of cheap writing paper. What I read scrawled across it turned me rigid with shock.

'We're going to get you, Yarwood,' I read, 'and by the time we've finished with you, you'll be unrecognisable ...' and so it went on, threatening to kill me and injure my family. It was signed 'The Angry Brigade'.

It was horrible. Much as I hate to give satisfaction to the sick people responsible by admitting it, I believed what they said and was very, very worried. I called the local police, who in turn called the Special Branch and eventually they came to the conclusion it was a hoax.

'You wouldn't be a target for the Angry Brigade,' they said. 'Besides, if someone was out to get you, they'd get you. They wouldn't warn you first. This is someone who wants to scare you. Probably someone who's jealous.'

I couldn't accept that. I couldn't imagine who could be so jealous as to do such a dreadful thing. But if someone wanted to scare me, they succeeded.

I was all right on stage. Strangely enough I felt safe on stage being appreciated by the audience. It was during the day that I felt bad, and when I was on my own, late at night. If somebody tapped me on the shoulder I jumped a mile.

Over the years with all the sociable winding-down drinks I'd taken after performances, I'd started to drink quite heavily without even realising it. Now, with the strain of the threat on my life and the loneliness of being on my own, I drank more than ever before. Until then I hadn't noticed how tired I was. I'd gone from pantomime to television series to summer season without a break, and for the first time since I'd come into show business I felt exhausted.

A drink seemed to perk me up for a couple of hours, but when it wore off I felt worse than ever. I longed to sleep, but when I lay down in bed I found I was listening to every squeak and creak and wondering if someone was trying to break in.

By the time Sandra came home I was in a terrible state, and the doctor ordered me to rest.

'Take a couple of weeks off and do absolutely nothing,' he said.

The theatre manager was wonderful. He rang me every day to see how I felt and was most considerate.

'Don't worry about it, Mike,' he said. 'Come back when you're ready.'

So I sat in the garden for a fortnight watching the flowers grow. The weather was terrific but I realised how jumpy I'd become the day a strange car containing two men pulled into the drive. I almost shot indoors in horror.

'Don't worry,' they called, 'we're from the *Sunday Mirror*.' That's almost worse than somebody wanting to get rid of me, I thought.

However, two weeks resting in the sun did me a lot of good and I was able to go back to the show as if nothing had happened. I'd more or less convinced myself that the letter was a hoax, but all the same it wasn't very nice knowing that someone out there hated me. Possibly even someone I knew. It was a chilling feeling.

I tried to push it out of my mind, along with a remark that the doctor had made when he ordered me to rest.

'I'll tell you something else,' he'd said, 'you're drinking too much.'

I didn't think I drank any more than the other people I knew and I didn't see why I should change. I continued to spend more time than I should in the BBC club or the pub. I'm working hard, I thought; I'm entitled to it. It didn't occur to me that I was behaving like a single man and that I left Sandra on her own more than I should have done.

By now I was becoming quite well known. I should have been delighted. I'd dreamed of fame all my life, but somehow when it came it wasn't as good as I'd expected.

There were amusing moments, of course. One night as I was leaving the Coventry Theatre after a show a woman clutching a little boy by the hand came over.

'Would you sign my programme for me, Mike?' she asked.

'Certainly,' I said.

'We love your show on Saturday nights,' she went on as I scribbled. 'At eight o'clock everything stops in our house for you.'

'That's very nice. Thank you,' I said. 'Very kind of you.'

'Mind you,' she added, taking the autographed programme, 'there's not much on ITV at the time.'

On another occasion a man thrust an autograph book under my nose.

'Would you sign this book?'

'Yes. What name is it, please?'

'Your name,' said the man.

'No, who should I sign it to?'

'To me,' said the man.

In the end I just scrawled Mike Yarwood and left it at that.

It's funny how people misunderstand you. They also tend to get mixed up and are convinced they know your past bookings better than you do.

'I saw you in 1967 at the North Pier, Blackpool, with Jimmy Clitheroe,' one man insisted as I signed an autograph.

'No, I wasn't there in 1967,' I explained politely. 'I was at the Britannia Pier, Great Yarmouth.'

'No, no, you weren't,' he said. 'You were at the North Pier, Blackpool with Jimmy Clitheroe. I remember distinctly.'

'But I've never been to the North Pier,' I explained. 'I've worked the Queens Theatre and the Central Pier, but never the North Pier.'

He wouldn't believe me. He was convinced that he'd seen me in 1967 in Blackpool and that if I didn't remember it was because the booking had slipped my mind. Nothing I could say would convince him that his memory was at fault.

Sometimes it was very nice being spotted by the public. Once I was sitting in a hotel lobby waiting for someone who'd been delayed. If there's one thing I detest, it's waiting in a public place for someone to join me. Anyway, I waited and waited and after a while two or three people came over.

'Just wanted to say how much we enjoyed the show,' they said pleasantly, 'but we'll let you have your coffee in peace.'

'No, that's OK,' I said, glad to have someone to talk to, and I tried to prolong the conversation. We talked for some time and I enjoyed it very much. Afterwards I thought how nice the incident had been. Had I not been famous I would have sat there alone and no one would have approached me. When they've seen you on television people think they know you and it's like having acquaintances all over the country.

But there are drawbacks. People can also be extremely rude. I was sitting one day with someone quite famous when a man approached us.

'I'd like your autograph,' he said brusquely to my companion. Then he recognised my face. 'Oh, and I might as well have yours too,' he added as if he was doing me a favour.

On another occasion I arrived back at my hotel after a show, tired and longing for bed. I picked up my key at reception and was heading for the lift when a man suddenly grabbed my arm.

'Come over here and meet my wife,' he said, trying to drag me across the lobby.

I was very annoyed. I was exhausted and I hate being grabbed like that.

'Why don't you bring your wife over here?' I felt like saying, but I bit my tongue. You never know – his wife might have been in a wheelchair.

As it happened she was fit and able-bodied. I signed an

autograph and got away as quickly as I could but I was furious at such rudeness.

Over the years it got worse and worse. Even when people didn't approach me, I could feel them staring. Wherever I went it felt as if eyes were following me. It was strange because I've never minded people looking at me when they're supposed to be, when I'm on stage, but when I'm not working I hate it.

The last straw came when I was visiting my mother in Bredbury and children kept peeping in the window at us. It might sound trivial but it felt as if I couldn't have privacy anywhere. Even driving my car I noticed people craning through the windows when I stopped at the traffic lights.

In the end I found I hardly wanted to leave the house except to go to work or visit friends. Sandra would have liked me to go round the supermarket with her and do the things other husbands did, but I couldn't face it.

'Why d'you assume people are going to be looking at you?' she used to say. 'It's pure conceit.'

'No, it's not; it's human nature,' I would reply. One year we took a rare holiday, to America (we went away only twice throughout our marriage), and while we were in Hollywood we kept seeing stars all over the place. I looked across a coffee bar one morning and saw Steve McQueen. I'd been staring for some time before I realised what I was doing, and that I was as bad as everyone else. It's just unpleasant when you're on the receiving end, and makes you feel uncomfortable; you can't relax in public places.

As the 1970s wore on I found myself staying at home more and more and my old childhood shyness came creeping back. Whenever possible when I did a summer season I rented a house and Sandra and the girls came to stay, but it was always Sandra who took the children to the beach or out on picnics. I couldn't face the crowds. One of my great regrets now is that

I didn't spend more time with my daughters when they were small, but I couldn't seem to get over this hang-up.

Perhaps things would have been different if I'd taken a job out of the public eye where I could have stayed anonymous. I'm pretty sure that if I had, my childhood shyness would have remained a thing of the past. In many ways I probably picked the worst possible profession for someone like me.

Not long ago Sandra and I went to a gymkhana to watch Clare ride and we hadn't been there five minutes when I was asked to present the prizes.

'You see what I mean, Sandra,' I said after I'd declined as politely as I could. 'It's not conceit. I just want to be like all the other dads, but people won't let me.'

Success of course was wonderful. People liked my shows and I loved reading the marvellous things that were written about me. But even success has a less pleasant side. Once you do a great show you have to follow it with an even greater show or a sensational one. You can never slip back. The pressure builds up and up. You have to prove yourself every time and the more successful you are, the more willing the critics are to knock you down.

It would have helped if I'd had a hobby to take my mind off work, but I didn't. I tried golf for a year or two but I never really got on with it. I wasn't very good and I don't like doing things unless I'm good at them. People used to say 'It's only a game.' And of course it is. But I can't enjoy playing a game if I'm hopeless at it, and what's the point of playing if it's not fun to do?

The answer to all my problems was a drink. At least I thought it was. Gradually I found I preferred drinking to eating. It became so noticeable to Max Bygraves that it became a running gag between us and one day after I'd picked my way through an unwanted meal he sent me a picture of a succulent roast dinner complete with meat, roast potatoes and two veg, which he'd cut from a magazine.

'This is food, remember?' he wrote on an accompanying note. 'And my advice is to eat it. It's good for you.'

A week or two later, quite by chance, I came across a magazine picture of an empty plate with a knife and fork resting on it and I cut it out and sent it to Max.

'It was delicious,' I wrote; 'thank you very much.'

At the time I thought it was funny, but in fact the situation was getting serious and I was making Sandra unhappy.

I'd become what the papers euphemistically describe as a 'hellraiser'. In fact I wasn't really wild. I never misbehaved or smashed things up or got into fights. I wasn't a doer. I just got 'tired and emotional' – another euphemism. Drink made me repetitive and boring and there were times when I said things I regretted afterwards.

By now I had a road manager, Bob Boyce, to look after me. I think I was quite a handful.

Sometimes we'd get back to the hotel late at night and Bob would head in a direction I didn't want to go.

'Bob, I want to go in the lounge,' I'd say.

'No, let's go downstairs and have a drink,' Bob would say, steering me towards the lift.

Years afterwards he told me that on these occasions he'd spotted the late Keith Moon, whose drinking sessions were legendary, in the lounge with his friends.

'I couldn't let you get with Keith Moon,' he said. 'You were bad enough on your own but you and Keith Moon – no.'

I never did meet Keith Moon. It was probably just as well. My worst fault (apart from being boring when I was drinking was that I didn't want the evening to end. I always wanted to go on somewhere else. I was much more sociable when I was drunk.

By 1976 I was feeling bad. I was signed up to do a season at the Victoria Palace Theatre in London. The show was called *The Time of your Life* and I think it was the worst time of my life. As well as doing two shows a night, I was also trying to make three TV shows during the day. They say that hard work never killed anybody – well, I think that cliché is completely untrue.

To make matters worse, an IRA bomb compaign was at its height in London. There were bomb scares everywhere – we had them at the theatre practically every night. Half the time I wasn't even told when there'd been a threat in case it put me off my act, but I was tense anyway. The public had been warned not to come into the city unless it was absolutely necessary, and you couldn't help but wonder if the place where you worked might be the next target.

It's bound to be a hoax, I'd tell myself every time I discovered another threat at the theatre, but part of me couldn't help thinking, yes, but what if it isn't?

On the last night there was a bomb scare at the end of the show, just as I was finishing my act. I was playing Columbo, the scruffy detective created by Peter Falk, and half-way through the impression I was interrupted.

'Ladies and gentlemen, we've had a telephone call to say that there's a bomb in the theatre. For your own safety could you please clear the building.'

There was an irritated sigh from the audience, a typically British reaction. No one seemed alarmed, there was no panic; they were just annoyed that the evening had been cut short. Unhurriedly they rose from their seats and filed out.

I stood frozen on the stage in a Columbo pose.

'Come on, Mike,' called Bob from the wings; 'we've got to get out of here.'

I walked out of the stage door, climbed into the car and rode all the way back to the hotel as Columbo, cracking Columbo gags. Dressed in the crumpled raincoat it seemed natural to stay in character.

My characters often came to the rescue in difficult moments. One night there'd been a muddle with a ticket agency and thirty-five tickets had been sold twice (a very rare occurrence, I hasten to add). The first I knew of it was when I walked on at the beginning of the show to find a commotion going on in the stalls. I was doing Larry Grayson at the time but the attention of the audience was diverted.

'You're sitting in our seats,' thirty-five standing people were telling thirty-five seated people.

'No, we're not, they're our seats.'

'No, they're not, we've got tickets.'

'So have we.'

Tickets were being waved in all directions and the situation was getting out of control. As Mike Yarwood I would have been in a fix, but Larry Grayson coped perfectly.

'Look,' he said from the stage, 'I can guarantee at least one of you a seat.'

My one Larry Grayson prop was a chair. He used to drag it on with him and lean on it as he talked. So I handed the chair across the footlights to the man nearest me and he played along by putting it in the aisle and sitting on it. We got a good laugh from the audience, then the manager arrived to smooth the situation.

There was one highlight during my season at the Victoria Palace and that was meeting Douglas Bader. He came backstage one night after the second show to say how much he'd enjoyed the evening.

He must have been getting on a bit then but it was impossible to tell how old he was. He was very alert and energetic and didn't appear handicapped in any way. I remember he smoked a short pipe and as he took the matches out to light it, he dropped them. Quickly I bent down to pick them up but he beat me to it. He was faster and probably fitter than I was.

It was a real thrill to meet the great man, who was one of the heroes from my schooldays.

'Wonderful show,' said Bader; 'how many times do you perform it?'

'Twice a night,' I explained.

'You perform two shows a night? I don't know how you do it,' he said, seeming genuinely impressed, and I've cherished his words ever since.

'I don't know how you do it.' Sometimes I wondered myself. The tiredness I'd first experienced at Scarborough returned, but worse than ever before. I felt tired all the time and it bothered me because I'm paranoid about being tired when I'm working. I hate to begin a show when I'm floppy and sluggish through lack of sleep. The more I worried about being tired, the more exhausted I became. I got to sleep well enough and I slept late, but it was that shallow half-sleep that doesn't seem to refresh you. I woke up even more tired than when I went to bed, and stayed tired all day.

At this time Sandra and I had our most miserable Christmas ever. In fact it was the worst Christmas I've ever spent in my life. I was appearing in a show on Christmas Eve and a show on Boxing Day and I couldn't face racing back to Prestbury on Christmas morning for one day. In the end we agreed that the girls would spend Christmas with their grandparents and Sandra would join me in my hotel.

The disaster was partly my fault. I was having a minor economy drive at the time and was trying to save money by staying in cheaper hotels when I worked away from home. On this occasion I was booked into a dreadful place in Ealing. There was no room service so at lunchtime Sandra and I went downstairs for our Christmas lunch.

'Have you booked a table, sir?' asked the waiter.

'No,' I said, 'but I'm a guest.'

'I'm sorry sir; if you haven't booked a table you can't have Christmas dinner.'

'But I've been staying here for weeks.'

'I'm sorry, sir. There's nothing I can do. The restaurant's full.'

I was almost too tired to care. We returned to our room where I dozed off again and slept right through lunch, then Sandra and I watched television. There was no tree, no decorations, no Christmas food and we missed the children badly, so we escaped into the television schedule. The only bright point of the whole day was the fact that there was a good movie on that night – *Butch Cassidy and the Sundance Kid*.

Immediately after Christmas I gave up my economy drive and moved back into a good hotel in central London. It was more comfortable but somehow I didn't feel a lot better.

Looking back I suppose it didn't help that I was so unfit physically. I saw a programme about a great actor recently. He worked incredibly hard but every day he went to the gym to keep in condition. To work hard you've got to keep fit, but I didn't know that then. I wasn't playing golf or tennis or doing exercises; I wasn't getting any fresh air; and I was drinking heavily. No wonder I didn't feel well.

I began to get depressed. What's the point of having this lovely house in Cheshire if I can't live in it and enjoy it? I asked myself. I live in hotels all the time. You can't have a big house if you don't earn the money to pay for it, came the answer, and you can't earn the money by staying at home.

It was a vicious circle.

But the worst of my problems was undoubtedly my drinking. Twice Sandra threatened to leave me but I managed to talk her out of it. Yet drink had begun to affect my life. I think it was Richard Burton who said that he knew that enough was enough when the hangovers stopped. Many people don't understand what he meant by that but I do. The normal guy who gets drunk says, 'Never again,' but the problem drinker will say, 'I need another drink!' Drink becomes its own antidote and if you don't have a drink you get withdrawal symptoms.

One day the hangovers stopped for me. It was the first of many dreadful, dreadful mornings when I needed a drink to stop the pain. If I couldn't get a drink I took valium, which the doctor had prescribed to help me cope with stress. Later I took valium as well as alcohol. Now of course everyone knows you should never mix tranquillisers with alcohol, but that's how stupid I was.

The only time I didn't drink was before a show. I was always very careful to remain absolutely sober when I was working. Some instinct for survival stopped me from ruining my career, but drinking affected just about every other area of my life. I couldn't understand why this should happen to me. My father and other members of my family had enjoyed a drink now and then without any problems, so why should I be different?

In the end, however, I felt so ill that I was forced to admit what Sandra and the doctor had been telling me all along. I drank far too much and I would have to stop.

I gave up drinking, but even then I was foolish. I believed that I couldn't get to sleep without a drink, so to help me over this problem, the doctor prescribed sleeping pills. I took sleeping pills for five years and sometimes I woke in the morning and found the glass of water and the pills still there beside me on the bedside table.

Instead of saying to myself, 'Look, that proves you don't need those bloody things,' I thought, 'Oh dear, I mustn't forget to take them tonight.' And I carried on taking them. It was crazy.

These days, thank goodness, I don't take sleeping pills or valium and I only drink occasionally. Quite honestly I'm scared of the stuff. I drink now and again to be sociable but I don't go on great all-night sprees after the show any more. Apart from anything else, at my age I don't have the stamina.

Now I go in for safer addictions. I can't pass a chocolate bar or an Indian restaurant without being tempted. In fact I daren't even think about Indian restaurants or I have to go out for a curry!

CHAPTER 10

Impressions
of Royalty

'We was so delighted back home, Michael, when we heard that you'd become a lord,' said an old Irish aunt of mine recently.

'Well no, Auntie, not quite a lord,' I explained.

Of course she was referring to my OBE. Much as I hated the 1970s I can't pretend the decade was one of unrelieved misery. Many good things happened during those years and one of the nicest was receiving the OBE.

It was the summer of 1976 when I received a letter from Downing Street. This wasn't in itself a staggering occurrence because my work brought me into contact with many politicians including prime ministers and ex-prime ministers, but nevertheless it was special enough to make me rip open the envelope immediately.

First my eyes swept to the signature at the bottom of the letter. It was from Harold Wilson. In rising excitement I started at the top again and skimmed the contents. I took in something about getting the Order of the British Empire.

The Order of the British Empire? That's the OBE, I thought.

'Sandra!' I yelled. 'I've been given an OBE.'

It blew my mind. The birth of Charlotte was still definitely the best moment of my life, but the OBE came a close second. It was like my first Palladium and my first Royal Variety show rolled into one. All I had to do was fill in the attached form with my name, age and occupation and return it to Downing Street. If I wanted to decline the honour I need only ignore the form.

I was torn between great excitement and the fear that it might be an elaborate hoax.

'Why me?' I asked Sandra. 'There are so many more deserving people than me.'

'Yes, but a lot of show business people get OBEs these days,' said Sandra. She was delighted but not as surprised as I was.

So I completed the form, sent it back almost by return of post and waited for the big moment. It took a long time to arrive. I hadn't realised that all the names on the birthday honours list, the new year's honours list and this one, Harold Wilson's resignation honours list, are added together then a number of investitures are carried out throughout the year in alphabetical order. Being a 'Y' I was naturally at the end of the queue, just as I'd always been at school, and it was winter before my turn came.

I was allowed to take three guests to Buckingham Palace with me: I would have loved to take my parents and Sandra, of course, but it was out of the question that my parents should go. My mother's illness had become so bad by now that she hardly ever left the house and my father, who had retired, stayed constantly at her side. A trip to London was quite impossible for them.

Instead, Sandra and I took Charlotte and Clare.

It was a wonderful experience. I felt nervous, of course, but very, very proud. We walked through a side door at the Palace into a splendid corridor, all red carpets and white and gold walls, past a line of horse guards so still you'd have sworn they were statues standing there.

'Daddy, are they real?' whispered Charlotte.

We assured her they were, but the men were so impossibly motionless she looked doubtful.

It was a sunny day and the guards looked magnificent with the winter sunshine striking their gleaming armour. Like all children the girls were fascinated by them, and they didn't really want to go when their names were called out and they were led away to the guests' seats in the main ballroom where they were to watch the investiture.

I was sent in another direction with the rest of the recipients.

First we were briefed on what to do. You entered the ballroom, stood well back, bowed and moved forward when the Queen spoke to you. After receiving the award you were allowed to turn your back on the Queen in order to see where you were going as you walked off, but at the end of the platform, you turned back to the Queen and bowed once more, before stepping down into the audience and sitting in the recipients' enclosure to watch the rest of the ceremony.

As a performer I'm used to taking stage directions so despite the fact that I was more nervous than I'd ever been before a Royal Variety Show, I didn't find it difficult. If only they'd given me a script as well it would have been perfect! I got the movements right but the dialogue was a disaster.

When my turn came I got through the obligatory bow well enough and approached the Queen without falling over. She was looking less formal than she'd done previously when she shook my hand at the Royal Gala. That was an evening engagement of course, when she'd been wearing a long dress, tiara and the works. Today she was smart but not ostentatious in a day dress and the minimum of jewellery.

'What are you doing at the moment, Mr Yarwood?' she asked as she shook my hand.

'I'm recording a new series for the BBC, ma'am,' I said, and in my nervousness I started to gabble, gathering momentum as

I went along until eventually I gave her my whole diary for the next year. I could hear myself running on but I couldn't seem to stop until I reached December when thankfully my memory failed me.

The Queen listened patiently and pinned the little blue and red ribbon to my chest. Then she nodded to show that the moment was at an end.

Why did I waffle on so much? I thought, mortified, as I walked off, almost forgetting to bow. But afterwards Sandra put my mind at rest by telling me that other people had talked for much longer than I did. I suppose the Royal Family must get used to terrified people babbling at them incoherently.

I sat in the space reserved for the recipients to watch the rest of the investiture. Then I met up with Sandra and the girls.

It was quite a while before we left the Palace because there were dozens of pictures to pose for and quotes to give the journalists gathered outside, but at last we were able to get away for a celebration lunch.

It was a lovely day and receiving the OBE was a great honour. However, since then I've been unsure as to how to use my award. I don't want to devalue it and make myself look pretentious by writing OBE everywhere at the end of my name, so in practice I don't use the letters much, but the little medal in its special box stays close at hand in my office and I look at it now and again to remind myself of that marvellous occasion.

In fact the investiture wasn't my first visit to Buckingham Palace. I had been invited there once before to a reception for the Lord's Taverners Association in the presence of Prince Charles, the Association's president. At the time I was driving a foreign car and the invitation threw me into a mild panic. There's no way I'm turning up at Buckingham Palace in a foreign car, I thought.

It sounds hypocritical because I've owned quite a few

foreign cars but I've always felt vaguely guilty about it. They have been very good cars and I've enjoyed driving them, but I'm very patriotic and deep down I feel I should always buy British.

Anyway I didn't want to arrive at Buckingham Palace in anything but a British car so I hired a Rolls Royce for the occasion. It was a bit ridiculous really because I was working at the Victoria Palace at the time, no more than five minutes away, and I could probably have walked there more quickly, but I could no more face walking through those huge gates and across that enormous expanse of gravel than I could driving in in a foreign car.

It was all very grand. The chauffeur whisked me past the crowds hanging round the railings and we were directed through the gate and the archway into the quadrangle, then on to the right where we parked the car. The bomb scare was still at its height in London and security was very tight. Security guards lifted the boot of the car and had a good look round it. Then I was free to set off up the steps into the Palace.

To my relief, in front of me I saw Ronnie Corbett, heading in the same direction.

'Oh Ronnie, am I glad I've seen you,' I said, catching him up. It was somebody to walk in with, apart from which I like Ronnie Corbett.

'And I'm glad I've seen you,' he said. 'I've come without a comb. Have you got one I could borrow?'

'Yes, of course.'

We walked into the Palace and headed straight for the toilets. To our surprise they were perfectly ordinary toilets, quite nice but nothing special. We'd been expecting crystal chandeliers and solid gold fittings and we couldn't help laughing about it. Later when I took Charlotte and Clare to the investiture they declared that the toilets at the Royal Garden Hotel were plusher! I don't know why we've all got this interest in royal loos, but I noticed that nearly everyone present visited them and half the time I'm sure it was more a pretext to see inside than because they needed to go.

Ronnie Corbett combed his hair then we went back outside. The corridor was full of commissionaires in lounge suits, who were wonderful. They treated us like particularly special house guests, making us very welcome. At no time did we feel we didn't belong. It was as if the Palace was part of our heritage and we had every right to be there.

The commissionaires called us sir, apologised for interrupting our conversation and directed us quietly to the reception. Ronnie and I stared around, determined to make the most of everything, because we might not be there again. The walls weren't gold encrusted or studded with jewels, but there were magnificent carpets everywhere and beautiful paintings on the walls. It was very impressive, more like a museum than someone's home, but then the Royal Family don't live in the rooms used for public occasions.

We were ushered into the reception, our names were announced and we were presented to Prince Charles.

'Are you a cricketer?' Prince Charles asked me.

'No sir, I'm not.'

He peered a little closer, then said, 'Oh yes, I know who you are.' For a second I thought he was merely being polite, but then he added, 'I hope you're not going to start bloody well doing me!'

He had a mischievous look on his face and there was something about the way he said it. I wondered whether he meant don't you dare mimic me, or whether it was an invitation to start.

To me it sounded like the latter and I got to work on my impression of Prince Charles soon afterwards. Until that moment it hadn't even occurred to me to mimic a member of the Royal Family. I'd always thought of them as being out of bounds. In fact until a few years ago you hardly ever saw cartoons of the Royal Family in newspapers although they're full of them today. Now to anyone who thinks that my impressions are disrespectful I can only say that it was Prince Charles himself who put the idea into my head.

In fact he is very difficult to do. I worked very hard to capture him but to this day I don't think I've got him quite right. He doesn't have many mannerisms to latch on to, and there's an elusive quality about his voice. However, I believe I have improved the impression over the last few years. I'm told that after one Royal Variety Show in which I included a Prince Charles sketch, the Queen turned to someone in the Royal Box and said, 'He's doing him better than he used to.'

I don't think Prince Charles minds. On one occasion I was asked to do the bingo at a charity dinner and I found myself seated at Prince Charles's table.

'What are you doing this evening?' he asked me.

'I'm doing the bingo, sir,' I said.

'Are you going to be me?'

'No, I think it would be pointless,' I explained. 'If I got up there and did you, everybody would start looking at you to see your reaction and they'd miss the impression.'

He didn't show it but I think the Prince was a little disappointed. He's got such a good sense of humour I think he enjoys watching impressions of himself.

Eating a meal with a member of the Royal Family is a daunting prospect, but the Prince put everyone at their ease. Sandra was actually sitting next to him and he asked her if I practised my impression of him at home.

'Oh yes,' said Sandra, 'in fact I've been living with you for the last three weeks.'

'I wish I'd known!' said Prince Charles. 'Does he do you as well?'

'Sometimes,' she replied.

This was true. Although I don't do women in my act I used to mimic Sandra to make her laugh when she was cross, just as years earlier I used to mimic my mother.

If Sandra found it an ordeal eating dinner with the Prince, she didn't show it. She did very well, laughing and joking without a trace of nervousness. When I got up to do the bingo, Prince Charles asked her how you played it.

'Well, sir,' said Sandra, amazed, 'you cross off the numbers as they're called out and the first one to complete all the numbers on their card is the winner.'

During the meal we were served fish on the bone and I was fascinated to see how the Prince dealt with it. At one point he got a bone in his mouth. He was talking, then he skilfully manoeuvred his fork and the bone was on the side of his plate in one graceful movement.

I was full of admiration. I've tried it since and it's not easy. They didn't teach you that sort of thing at the school I went to.

I've found the only way to cope in situations like this is to watch what royalty are doing and copy it, but this course of action doesn't cover every hazard. One of my most embarrassing moments occurred during a meal with Princess Margaret.

I'd been invited to a Dr Barnado's luncheon at which Princess Margaret was the guest of honour, and I found I was sitting next to her.

The Princess was charming and I was just beginning to relax when the main course was served. It was lamb chops. These can sometimes be very difficult to cut, especially if the knives aren't as sharp as they might be. Anyway, I was talking away to Princess Margaret when suddenly my knife slipped, the lamb chop flew off my plate and into orbit. I could only stare in horror as it sailed across the tablecloth and came to rest a few inches in front of my place-setting in a great splodge of dark brown gravy.

Just thinking about it makes me cringe even now. The

Princess was wonderful. She immediately turned away as if nothing had happened and started talking to the person on her other side. This gave me time to retrieve the chop, put it back on my plate and cover the gravy with a napkin. By the time she turned back everything was clean and orderly again and fifty per cent of my embarrassment had been extinguished. The remaining fifty per cent was pretty powerful though.

After that I left the chops untouched and ate only the softer vegetables. I've regarded lamb chops as dangerous fare ever since.

The Royal Family seem to be able to handle any situation perfectly. Everything they do is absolutely correct. In my own very small way I can understand a little of what it must be like for them. I'm sometimes asked to open a fête or visit a hospital and I know how tough it is sometimes to keep the conversation going. Members of the Royal Family are experts in this difficult field.

I remember after one Royal Variety Show, a member of the Royal Family (I won't say who) asked me about the little rat-shaped badge I was wearing in my lapel.

I'd been made a member of the Grand Order of Water Rats, the show business brotherhood, in 1968, and the little rat is the emblem of the order. I wear it on all important show business occasions. Anyway, I explained this to the member of the Royal Family and she listened intently, apparently very interested in a topic quite new to her.

After the presentation the performers relaxed and I fell into conversation with Danny La Rue who is also a Water Rat.

'What did she say to you, Danny?' I enquired.

'Oh, she asked about the little rat I was wearing in my lapel.'

Now Danny had been standing further down the line, so I know for a fact that by the time she reached him she'd already had at least one very full explanation of the significance of the rat emblem, yet she had listened to Danny's version with as much interest as she'd listened to mine. I expect she'd encountered the water rat on many many previous occasions but it was a good topic of conversation and she used it skilfully as a prop to help the discussion along.

I've been privileged to meet several members of the Royal Family and the least typically 'royal' of them all was Princes Diana. She is a beautiful girl and very well spoken but without that distinctive 'royal' accent. She's also more open than the older members of the family, with the exception of the Queen Mother. I expect this is because she was brought up in a more relaxed atmosphere.

I was presented to Princess Diana at a special show to mark the opening of the Barbican Centre in 1980. At this time I'd been experimenting with a new Charles and Diana sketch. I played Prince Charles and actress and comedienne Suzanne Danielle played Princess Diana. Suzanne is very dark, but she put on a blonde wig and ended up looking remarkably like the Princess. We set the scene in the couple's home and had them chatting together like any other husband and wife.

The idea was an immediate success with the public and Suzanne and I had many requests to repeat it, but the newspapers claimed that the Queen was not amused.

I found it very difficult to believe this was true. The whole thing seemed so harmless I couldn't imagine how anyone could take offence. The sketch took place in the Prince and Princess's kitchen at breakfast time and contained a lot of visual gags, such as a tea cosy with a crown on it.

The best joke of all concerned the fridge.

'I wish people would just occasionally treat us like ordinary people,' Charles said to Diana. 'Why do they behave as if we're special? I mean, there's nothing special about us, is there?'

And he opened the fridge and a flunkey's hand came out and passed him a bottle of milk.

The couple went on to discuss their day and Princess Diana

mentioned that she had got a Welsh lesson booked, and so on and so on.

It seemed very innocent to me and I couldn't imagine that Prince Charles for one had objected to it. Nevertheless after the fuss in the press I wondered what sort of reaction I would get when I met the couple at the Barbican.

It was a long show with a sixty-minute interval during which the cast was to be presented to the Prince and Princess. I was doing two spots, one in each half. I opted for President Reagan during the first and since I'd received a specific request through my agent that I include a Prince Charles impression, I saved that for my second spot. To be on the safe side I steered clear of the Charles and Diana sketch.

'Are you going to do him?' asked Princess Diana when she reached me, swivelling her eyes to indicate Prince Charles who was moving down the line behind her. She was looking so radiant and lovely that everybody else looked old beside her.

'Oh yes,' I said.

'And is your actress friend with you tonight?'

She was referring of course to Suzanne Danielle and what she was really asking was whether we were going to do the Charles and Diana sketch.

'No, I'm afraid I'm working on my own tonight,' I explained.

Like Prince Charles before her, Princess Diana didn't indicate whether or not she was disappointed.

'The first time I saw that sketch I laughed till I cried,' she said, 'and it takes a lot to make me cry laughing.'

I was knocked out. It was very nice of her to tell me and I was thrilled to think that the Waleses themselves were amused by the sketch. If they approved, then I didn't see how anyone else could object.

Strangely enough other people seem more than willing to take offence on their behalf. I once did a sketch in which

The things press photographers make you do! Here I'm arriving to see you-know-who.

Mum and Dad.

This is me at the Lobby Correspondents' Luncheon at the Savoy in 1981 with two of my scriptwriters.
(I'm the one without the pipe.)

Top: At the opening of the Barbican Centre in 1982
with Elaine Page and Princess Diana.

Above: Dunbar, Walton-on-Thames, Surrey.

Right: 'Tommy Steele'.

FRANKIE

This page:

Above left: 'Frankie Howerd' just getting himself comfy.

Above right: 'HRH'.

Right: 'Lionel Blair' (he's the one in the white suit).

Opposite page:

Above left: 'Sir Terry Wogan' at last.

Above right: The real Dennis Healey with his 'twin sister'.

Below left: 'Sir Richard Attenborough'.

Below right: 'It is, is it not, Russell Harty?'

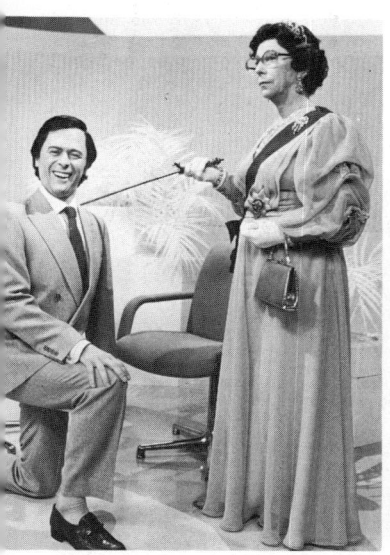

'Hello, good evening and welcome.'

'Bob Geldof' with Anneka Rice.

Above: 'Gorbachev'. *Below:* 'President Reagan'.

And finally ... Mike Yarwood.

Charles parked his car and the whole thing revolved around the fact that he didn't know how a parking meter worked. A traffic warden comes along and tries to give him a ticket but the Prince doesn't know what she's talking about. He's never even seen a parking ticket.

Afterwards I got an irate letter from a viewer complaining that I'd made Prince Charles out to be a buffoon. I wrote back explaining that she'd missed the point: I wasn't saying that Charles was a buffoon – merely that he was unfamiliar with parking meters.

The key point with my royal gags is that the Royal Family lead such different lives from ordinary people that they are baffled by things that we commoners take for granted. Perhaps I don't succeed, but I take care not to be disrespectful in my Prince Charles impressions. My main worry nowadays is that I might unwittingly have encouraged other people, who don't have the same scruples, to tackle the royal family. I hate to see a bad impression of Prince Charles, and it's awful to think that I might be to blame. Before I started doing him, I don't think anyone else had attempted it. Now I see quite a few impressions of him and they're not all in the best of taste.

Spitting Image is particularly worrying because it's so cruel, but perhaps the Royal Family don't mind. After all, they're used to seeing themselves caricatured in cartoons these days.

CHAPTER 11

Affairs of State

I should have known Ted Heath was going to get his revenge, before he even opened his mouth.

As he stood up to speak, he glanced in my direction, a mischievous look in his eye.

'My Lord Mayor, Your Excellency, My Lords, Gentlemen ...' he turned to me and gave a hint of a bow, 'Prime Minister and Leader of the Opposition ...'

Everyone laughed and I came over all embarrassed. I must have gone red, because Ted added:

'Look! He's actually blushing. He must be human after all!'

We were attending the Men of the Year Luncheon at the Savoy Hotel, but Ted was getting his own back for an incident that had occurred some years before.

In 1967 I was asked to do the cabaret at a celebration dinner at the Café Royal to honour round-the-world yachtsman Sir Francis Chichester. Ted Heath, a keen sailor, was the guest speaker at this function, but unfortunately he was delayed and walked in just as I was starting my Harold Wilson impression.

Everyone turned to watch his entrance and I stood there in my Harold Wilson raincoat, pipe clenched between my teeth.

It was the ideal moment for some apt ad-lib and my mind was racing. Then inspiration came. I silently watched as Ted Heath crossed the room and sat down and then in my Harold Wilson voice I said:

'I sincerely hope the latecomer hasn't come to heckle.'

There was a great roar of laughter which Ted joined in with, and for the first time I noticed that his shoulders shook when he laughed. From that day on I used the mannerism in my impression. Until then Ted hadn't been easy to capture. That rounded voice meant that I had to move my mouth a great deal and there didn't seem to be any physical detail to latch on to.

Suddenly I'd got one: I could make Ted a rather jovial figure and use the shaking shoulders to the full. From Ted's remark at the Savoy, however, I gathered that he wasn't very keen on it.

I found him a cold man: friendly, but in a distant way. We were introduced at the reception prior to the lunch.

'How d'you do,' said Ted politely.

'We have met before actually, Prime Minister,' I said, 'in 1967.'

'Oh no, I don't think so.'

'We did.'

'Oh no, I *don't* think so,' he said again in such a way that you didn't argue.

I was puzzled. I could understand that he might not remember meeting me, but I was unlikely to forget meeting the Leader of the Opposition.

Throughout the 1960s and early 1970s Harold Wilson and Edward Heath switched jobs, which made life quite easy for me. It didn't really matter which one was Prime Minister; each could insult the other and it still made sense.

Harold Wilson would say: 'When you die, Ted, I'm going to dance on your grave.'

'Good,' Ted would reply, 'I'm going to be buried at sea.'

In later years it was more of a problem. I remember in 1979 I was appearing in Norwich the day of the election results. My script was written as if James Callaghan had been elected Prime Minister, but just before I went on stage the news came through that Margaret Thatcher had won.

What the hell do I do now? I thought. If Callaghan's not Prime Minister, my script doesn't make sense. Then an idea began to come into my mind and when I came to my Callaghan spot, I abandoned the whole script. I substituted just one line:

'I demand a recount,' I said and started to cry. I stood there crying for about one and a half minutes. It brought the house down and it got me off the hook.

As well as getting the appearance and voice of a politican right, it was important to home in on a recognisable characteristic. With Wilson it was his ego.

'My name is Sir Harold Wilson, but you can call me sir ...'

'No please, don't get up. Treat me as an equal.'

'This morning I'm starting on the second volume of my memoirs then I don't quite know what I'm doing this afternoon.'

There was no ego with Edward Heath. I had to make do with the shaking shoulders and his fondness for the sea. Callaghan was difficult, too. There was nothing much to latch on to until the day he returned from abroad and pretended to know nothing of the chaos that had taken place in his absence.

'Crisis, what crisis?' he asked reporters when he arrived in the country.

After that I portrayed him as permanently believing that everything in the garden was lovely.

'Don't know what you're talking about. Strike? What strike?' 'Crisis in the Middle East? What crisis in the Middle East?'

There were also jokes like, 'We're not worried about education. Well, not as much as we was ...'

Mind you, there were places I worked where that line never got a laugh because they couldn't see what was wrong with it.

American presidents were presented as buffoons, although I always felt a little sorry portraying Jimmy Carter in that light because he seemed such a nice man. You couldn't help feeling sorry for him when things went wrong.

Some politicians were almost impossible. I couldn't get Sir Alec Douglas-Home, or former Liberal leader Jeremy Thorpe, at all. For years I've found it difficult to put the explanation for this into words but not long ago I heard a description that's exactly right. 'His personality wasn't vivid,' an actor said when describing a well known personality. This sums it up beautifully: I can't capture people who are not vivid. That's the best way I can put it.

In the early days when I was doing my Wilson and Heath jokes they were not in the best of taste. I used to do one gag where Mary Wilson goes to the doctor for a check-up.

'You're in very good health, Mrs Wilson,' says the doctor, 'but I'm shocked and surprised to find that you're still a virgin.'

'Well, you know Harold,' replies Mary, 'promises, promises!'

And when I did Heath, I made him say;

'We in the Conservative Party are very proud to say you've never had it so good, but under this government, you've never had it. Lower cost of living? You've never had it. Better housing? You've never had it. And I as a bachelor never cease to wonder how I manage. I've never had – it ...'

These jokes got good laughs but I dropped them if the politician in question was in the audience, and later I dropped them altogether.

The only problem with including politicians in my act was that when there was an election pending I wasn't allowed to do them on television. Both the BBC and ITV would come down on you like a ton of bricks, and I had to leave out politicians until the election was over.

On the plus side, I found I was invited to the election night parties, not as a guest but to do the cabaret. Far from being offended, the politicians loved to see my impressions of their colleagues.

Harold Wilson used to make jokes apologising for the sketchiness of his speeches because, 'I've just written it on the back of a menu, being forced to use such time as I've left over from writing scripts for Mike Yarwood ...'

And Edward Heath himself declared, 'If either of us should ever disappear under a bus, we have a ready-made substitute without the expense of an election!'

Harold himself made it clear, when I finally met him in Blackpool where he was attending the annual Labour Party Conference and I was in summer season, that he regarded me as one of the best public relations men he ever had.

Dennis Healey agreed.

'People smile at me now,' he said. 'They didn't in the past. You make me look like some kind of lovable uncle!'

The strange thing was that for years I'd been inventing characters for my politicians, yet when I eventually met them they were exactly as I'd imagined. For example, I felt as if I'd known Harold Wilson for years (in a way I had I suppose).

No matter who I'm doing, it's much better to meet them personally that to watch them on television. I like to get as close to them as possible. I study their features, listen carefully to their voices and generally scrutinise them as minutely as I dare without appearing rude. I remember once at a function at Downing Street I got so close to Jim Callaghan that I noticed the pale stripes in his smart pin-striped suit weren't ordinary stripes at all, but tiny rows of initials. Each stripe was in fact made up of hundreds of little 'J.C.'s, so minute and so tightly crammed together that they looked like a continuous line.

'I'll tell you something about that material,' said Jim when I remarked on it; 'it was a gift from Jimmy Carter.'

Apparently the fabric had been given to President Carter and he had some over, so he thought he would pass it on to someone he knew with the same initials – Jim Callaghan.

This wasn't my first visit to Downing Street. I've been there several times to various functions and it's always struck me as being similar to Buckingham Palace in that it looks rather like a museum inside, and that the guests are treated with the same perfect hospitality. In one way, Number Ten is a bit like Dr Who's police box, The Tardis, because it's about four times as large inside as it appears from the outside. Like Buckingham Palace it is full of art treasures, on show to the visiting dignitaries, and it also contains portraits of every British prime minister.

The garden is surprisingly large too, and once in the 1970s I was invited to a garden party there.

I remember the occasion chiefly because Eric Morecambe and Ernie Wise were also guests and it was a very funny afternoon. At one point a woman wearing a peculiar hat that made her look like a fish approached Eric.

'I'm sure I know you,' she said.

'Yes, I saw you on a slab at MacFisheries,' said Eric under his breath. Fortunately she didn't hear him.

Later in the afternoon Mary Wilson took me indoors and showed me photographs of her grandchildren. She had a great quality of serenity that I hadn't encountered since I was a child at the convent school. It may sound strange to describe the wife of the Prime Minister as being like a nun, but she had that same inner stillness I'd noticed in the nuns who used to teach me at school.

In fact, throughout our entire conversation it was difficult ro remember that I was talking to the Prime Minister's wife. Mary Wilson put on no airs at all, and she went through the photograph album like any other proud grandmother, no different really from the way my mother showed off the pictures of her grandchildren in her little house in Bredbury.

The biggest gathering I attended was the Lobby Correspondents' Annual Lunch. Everybody was there: every member of the cabinet and the opposition, past and present prime ministers. It made you wonder who was looking after the shop. It was amazing to see how the politicians mingled. Some people from opposing parties seemed to get on better with each other than they did with their political brothers.

At one point I was talking to Michael Foot, who was briefly leading the Labour Party. He was marvellous: all that bushy hair sweeping back, the rumpled clothes – I thoroughly enjoyed doing Michael Foot. It was just before the General Election which Margaret Thatcher won and he knew he was going to lose. He didn't say so, but you could tell he knew it.

'Margaret Thatcher's going to be a big problem for you, isn't she?' he said.

'With respect she's a bigger problem for you than she is for me,' I thought, but I didn't say it aloud. 'She's an incredible woman,' I said instead.

To my surprise Michael Foot agreed with me. He said how much he admired her as a politician. He didn't admire her policies but he thought she was a strong, able woman and he had great respect for her.

After the election, which was disastrous for Foot, Clive James named him as the politician of the year for soldiering on through the campaign when he knew he didn't have a hope. He could have winged it, but he soldiered on. I couldn't help admiring him myself and I felt rather sorry for him when he inadvertently caused a rumpus by wearing a donkey jacket to the Cenotaph on Remembrance Sunday.

'I thought I looked all right,' he said in bewilderment to a colleague afterwards.

He wasn't intending any disrespect. He genuinely felt that he looked presentable. The day I met him at the lobby correspondents' lunch, he had a stain on his suit. Possibly he hadn't had time to go home and change, but more likely he didn't even notice it. His mind was on other things.

Not long after my conversation with Michael Foot I was introduced to Mrs Thatcher. We talked polite chit-chat for a moment or two and I didn't have time to form an opinion of her, but I noticed that she had a very young face: close up there was no sign of age round her eyes. If you didn't know that she wasn't the type, you'd swear blind she'd had her face lifted.

She was very smart and clean-looking and like the Queen there was no hint of perfume from her.

Wandering round the reception I was able to hear all kinds of tantalising gossip.

'The trouble with Heath and Thatcher,' said one famous politician, 'is that they're poor people trying to run a rich firm.'

I wouldn't know about that but it's true they both came from relatively humble backgrounds.

When Margaret Thatcher became Prime Minister, I wondered, only half seriously, whether I should try to mimic her. Since I'd been impersonating prime ministers for so long the papers wanted to write a little story about the problems I might now have to face, and they persuaded me to pose for a jokey picture in a blonde 'Mrs Thatcher' wig.

But soon after the picture appeared, I gave up any ideas of putting her in my act. I couldn't get the voice at all, and in any case I've never been happy about mimicking women, except for a joke at home. The only 'women' I've ever done have been men in drag, like Danny La Rue and Barry Humphries as Dame Edna Everage.

Neil Kinnock wasn't a lot easier: apart from the Welsh accent there wasn't much for me to go on. All the same I tried, and not long afterwards I met Kinnock at the Labour Party Conference.

'I saw the impression, Mike, and the only thing wrong was the hair,' said Kinnock. 'There was too much hair on your head: I haven't got as much as that. Can I borrow your wig?'

I was surprised to find that talking to Kinnock was like talking to someone you'd meet in a rugby club. There were no ladies present and he used rugby club language and was really one of the boys. He didn't keep his distance as so many politicians do even when they're being friendly.

I spent a lot of time listening to Kinnock's speeches in an effort to capture his voice and I discovered that he is a marvellous speaker. It was almost irritating from my point of view because half the time I found myself listening to what he was saying instead of the way he was saying it.

I'm still not satisfied with my Kinnock impression but perhaps if he ever becomes prime minister I'll have rather more to go on.

David Steel isn't too bad from my point of view but David Owen has a difficult mouth. I'll have to do more work on them if the Liberal-SDP Alliance gets in at the next election.

Of all my politicians I think Harold Wilson has been the most successful. I certainly found him the easiest to mimic and he is popular to this day. I've done so many impressions of him that I think I've become associated with the Labour Party, and Ron Hayward, the party admissions secretary, once wrote to ask if I would like to join the special show business section. I declined as politely as I could: like the television companies I feel I should be impartial. No one forces me to give equal time in my act to each party, but I feel it wouldn't be right to have a bias in any particular direction.

Over the years I've always been made welcome by politicians and I think it's because I don't go for the jugular. Harold Wilson in particular seemed to appreciate my work. He gave me the OBE of course, and he also invited me on to a chat show once. He was the guest host of a programme called *Friday Night Saturday Morning* and he invited Robin Day, Winston Churchill and me to join him. There was one tricky moment during that show. It was filmed at the time when Joe Kagan, an acquaintance of Wilson's, had been discovered to be a crook. Kagan's company, Kagan Textiles, produced the Gannex raincoats that were almost Wilson's trade mark, and Wilson honoured Kagan with a knighthood, then a peerage.

Some time later Kagan's tricky dealings were uncovered, and he disappeared before the police could catch him. He was stripped of his knighthood, but nothing could be done about the peerage. It was highly embarrassing for Harold Wilson.

'Tell me, Mike,' said Wilson during the show, 'when you do me now I notice you don't wear the raincoat. Why's that?'

'We can't find the man who makes them,' I said without thinking.

It got a big roar from the audience but Wilson just looked, and passed on to another topic.

Afterwards Robin Day said to me, 'I thought that was a bit strong.'

'Well it got a big laugh,' I replied, but of course he was there to say something intelligent, not to get laughs, so I suppose we didn't see it in the same light.

Harold Wilson and I also appeared together on the *Parkinson Show*. Parky wanted Ted Heath as well but Ted declined. I didn't know whether it was me he wanted to avoid or Wilson or both! Harold Wilson had just retired and when I turned up at the run-through they were trying out the music they'd chosen to play as he walked on to the set. It was called 'The Party's Over'.

'Parky, you can't play that!' I said, though why I thought I should interfere I don't know. 'He'll know! This man is as sharp as a razor. He'll recognise that tune straight away and he'll say that's out for a starter.'

Parky relented and the music was changed: they played 'On Ilkley Moor baht 'at' instead.

The show went well, though I suffered from Wilson's disconcerting habit of apparently failing to hear a question in order to gain time to consider the answer. At one point I asked what percentage of the people in a general election vote for the prime minister and what percentage vote for their local MP.

There was silence and Harold Wilson went off on a left turn to say something to the person on the other side of him. I thought I'd got egg on my face, when suddenly he turned back and reeled off all the relevant figures.

And he couldn't resist a joke.

'Don't sit too close to me,' he said. 'I've got a stinking cold and I was hoping you could take over my engagements for the next week!'

CHAPTER 12

New Directions

As the 1970s came to an end and the 1980s began, I was on the verge of a complete change in my life, although I didn't realise it at the time. There were just two more surprises before my old life changed for good. They were both highlights in a way, although it may sound odd to call the theft of my car, which was one of the events, a highlight.

It was late in the summer of 1981 and I was staying at the Royal Garden Hotel, Kensington while I was rehearsing my TV show. Not long before I'd swapped my secondhand Rolls for a brand new model and it was my pride and joy. Dark red and gleaming, it cheered me up whenever I got depressed about the pressures of show business and the amount of time I had to spend away from home.

When I was staying at the Royal Garden, my road manager always parked the Rolls in the NCP underground car park beneath the hotel. It was a convenient arrangement and we'd never had any problems before, but this particular Friday night he came to my room with a worried look on his face.

'The car's gone,' he said.

'Gone?'

'Yes. I've searched the whole car park. It's gone. Stolen, I suppose.'

I was furious. My beautiful brand new Rolls Royce stolen. How could the car park people have let it happen? When I cooled down of course I realised they couldn't have prevented it. The police took down all the details and a description of the car and explained that I would just have to wait and see what happened – there was a chance they might recover it. All I could do in the meantime was hire a car to take me to the studios.

News of the car wasn't long in coming, and I was told that it had been found the next day. It had been used for a jewel robbery. Apparently the number plate, JCH 844V, had been changed to LSD 777, which was a cheeky touch. LSD stands for money and 777 is the jackpot line on many one-armed bandits. Having changed the plates, the gang had driven to Kutchinsky's, the exclusive jewellers in Bond Street, and, posing as wealthy customers, they'd walked into the shop, pulled out a gun and cleared almost the entire window display of platinum and diamond rings, necklaces and bracelets. The whole robbery took less than a minute.

It was obviously a well planned operation. Unfortunately for my Rolls, however, the gang's getaway driver was not so professional, or perhaps he wasn't familiar with the car. They shot off round the corner and hit a Jaguar! The two vehicles careered on down the street locked together, then the driver of my Rolls wrenched it clear and swerved away, bouncing off five other cars before speeding into the distance. Later the car was found abandoned a short distance away in Kingly Street, and the gang had escaped with half a million pounds worth of jewellery.

It's hard to smash up a car like a Rolls Royce. Any other car treated like that might well have been wrecked, but when I was taken to see my pride and joy I found only a broken radiator grille and scrapes along the sides.

Although I'd been annoyed at first, I soon found I was enjoying myself. The story was in all the papers and I was even on the news. Now normally I hate doing interviews but it was quite different being part of a news story: the whole thing was tremendously exciting, and I was surrounded by people clamouring for comments.

'Hang on BBC, I'll be with you in a minute,' I heard myself saying grandly; 'I'm on to ITV at the moment,' and although I've been on television so many times, I probably got more of a kick out of that than anything else.

Better still, the police needed my help. They were very apologetic but they wondered if I would mind going to the station to be fingerprinted so they could eliminate my prints from any they found on the car.

'Sorry to inconvenience you, sir.'

I was dumb-struck. 'Inconvenience me? I would love to come,' I said.

Women grow up but men never do, and I was like a kid again. It was just like being in *The Sweeney*, and I'm a cop-show fanatic at the best of times. They took my hand and put it on a pad of what looked like black ink.

'Relax,' said the policeman.

'I am relaxed,' I said.

'Right. Don't you press, I'll press,' he told me and pressed my hand down on to the black. Afterwards it was covered in dark smears but they washed off easily.

The police were pleased because they'd found a raincoat in the back of the car and they showed it to me.

'Is this your raincoat?' they asked.

'No,' I said, enjoying myself. As a cop-show addict I understood the significance of the find. If it belonged to the gang it would be full of clues and might even lead to an arrest.

Then I looked at the coat again. I wouldn't be seen dead in a scruffy thing like that of course, but there was something familiar about it. Then I remembered. I wouldn't wear a coat like that as myself, but when I was Columbo I did. It was my Columbo prop.

'Eh, sorry, that is my raincoat. I've just realised,' I said, embarrassed.

The police were terribly disappointed.

I don't think they ever did catch the jewel robbers but my car was soon as good as new. The Rolls Royce people came down, covered it up, whisked it away and returned it to me as if it had just come straight from the showroom.

Exciting though the whole episode had been, I didn't feel the same way about the car after that. It looked wonderful yet I felt it had been contaminated in some way and it wasn't long before I got rid of it.

The other highlight of this time was being the subject of *This is your Life*. It was genuinely a total shock. People always ask you if the subject is warned in advance; well, the answer is definitely no. Of course when you start to become fairly well known you can't help realising there's a chance you might be on *This is your Life*, and once before I'd even thought I was being set up for it. I'd been invited to appear on *The Russell Harty Show* which wasn't strange in itself because I'd been on chat shows before, but there did seem to be something odd about this particular occasion. For a start there seemed to be very little preparatory work done; no research that I knew of was carried out and I didn't even meet Russell Harty until we were in make-up. (Usually you meet the host before the show starts and discuss what you're going to do.)

This is obviously the way Russell Harty prefers to work, but it was so different from my past experiences that I began to doubt we were really doing a show at all. Russell can't really want to interview me, I thought, this must be a set up for something else. The only something else I could think of was *This is your Life*.

All through the interview I found it difficult to concentrate. I kept looking out for Eammon Andrews and waiting for those dreaded words, 'This is your life!'

They didn't come. Russell Harty wound up the interview, thanked me for coming and I was on my way out of the studio before I realised the truth – it had been a genuine interview after all. I only wished I'd paid more attention.

When *This is your Life* really happened I didn't have a clue, although looking back there were plenty of hints. For weeks beforehand Sandra rushed to the phone every time it rang and said, 'No, I'm sorry, you've got the wrong number.'

It happened so often that even I couldn't fail to notice it.

'What's the matter with the phone, Sandra?' I asked. 'All these wrong numbers. We'll have to get it checked.'

In fact it was a code to let the television team know that I was present and she couldn't talk.

Then there were the girls' dresses. Sandra had just finished making Charlotte and Clare new party frocks but about a week later she bought two more.

'Why do they need another two frocks?' I asked. 'Haven't you just made some?'

'Yes, but these were so nice I thought I might as well get them as well,' said Sandra. 'They have so many parties at this time of year.'

I didn't give it another thought. I wasn't at all suspicious, and Sandra let nothing slip. It must have been difficult for her because she's a very open person and can't lie, but she kept the secret brilliantly.

Nevertheless there were other odd occurrences. The *This is your Life* team needed an excuse to get me to London, since I was between television shows at the time, so suddenly my accountant was insisting I come to London for an urgent discussion of my finances, and my agent arranged an important business lunch for the same day. I agreed half-heartedly and travelled to London the evening before in order to be fresh the next day. Bob Boyce and I walked into the Royal Garden Hotel.

'Mike Yarwood; I've booked,' I said at the reception desk.

'Ah yes,' said the girl, 'Mr and Mrs Yarwood. Two nights.'

'No,' cut in Bob quickly. 'It's *Mr* Yarwood only, just for tonight!'

The girl looked confused, then blushed. Although I didn't know it she'd almost given the game away. A room had been booked for Sandra and me the following night after the show, at a time when I thought she would be safely at home in Prestbury and I would be travelling back to her.

'Oh yes, of course,' she said quickly, 'Mr Yarwood.'

The next day I went to the lunch as planned and then on to the Hilton Hotel for the meeting with my accountant. It seemed a perfectly ordinary day and I was glad when the business was finished and I could go home.

Bob and I made our way back through the Hilton towards the entrance where Bob knew that Eamonn Andrews and the television crew were waiting. We'd almost reached the door when I stopped.

'Oh, I must ring Sandra,' I said.

'Can't you call her later?' asked Bob, trying to move me towards the door.

'No, I always ring her when I'm leaving,' I said and back I went to find a phone.

With no idea of the havoc I was causing outside, I dialled our number at home and listened to it ringing and ringing. I tried it once again, just in case I'd misdialled, but the same thing happened.

'There was no reply,' I said to Bob a few minutes later, 'I expect she's out with the girls somewhere.'

Of course Bob knew that there was no reply because Sandra was at that moment sitting in the studios at Thames Television watching the outside of the Hilton Hotel on a monitor and waiting for me to step into the picture.

'Never mind, you can try again later,' said Bob, steering me towards the door once more.

Through the plate glass I suddenly saw Jimmy Tarbuck.

'There's Jimmy!' I said in surprise.

I quickened my pace and went to greet him.

'Hello, Jimmy!' I called, then stopped. Michael Parkinson was standing next to him, along with Russell Harty and Patrick Moore.

'Hello Mike, Hello Russell, Hello Patrick ... What's going on?'

'Oh, there's a do on,' said Jimmy.

There was always some charity function happening somewhere so this didn't seem unlikely. We started chatting – then suddenly Eamonn Andrews stepped out from behind me, clutching his famous red book. The instant I saw him my stomach started to churn.

'Mike Yarwood, this is your life!' said Eamonn.

'Aaaaaah ****...' – I was completely thrown and a four letter word escaped. Fortunately they bleeped it out afterwards.

It was an overwhelming experience. One minute I was going home, and the next thing I knew I was in a limousine travelling to the television studios at Euston. The whole thing is like your wedding day – it's so overpowering and goes by so fast that you can't remember much about it when it's over. Watching a video of the show afterwards was like watching someone else.

They showed clips of some of my impressions and brought the subjects into the studio. There was Magnus Pyke, Larry

Grayson, Reginald Bosanquet, Russell Harty and of course Michael Parkinson.

'When I watch him it's like watching another person,' said Larry Grayson, 'but then afterwards I realise it's me.'

'I never before said "you are, are you not" until Mike did it,' said Russell Harty.

'And I never started picking my nose until Mike did it,' said Michael Parkinson.

'I don't show you picking your nose,' I protested, laughing. 'I do you *rubbing* your nose.'

But there wasn't much time for discussion. They'd filmed my mother in Bredbury recalling the day I bought her a bath cube for her birthday when I was four; they'd flown David in from Africa where he was doing missionary work; and they'd tracked down so many old friends from the past. There was Neil Jenkins, a reliable Broadway Rover in the old days; Tommy Dunbar, who recalled our Mr Tacky and Mr Hacky sketches; Wilf Fielding; and of course Roy Mayoh. He turned up clutching the Ewbank carpet sweeper that had taught me so much about microphone technique.

'Mike, if you do really well one day I'll promote you to a Hoover!' he promised.

The Bachelors came on and joked, 'We always felt safe when we were working with Mike because if we got tired he could go on instead of us!'

Dilys Watling recalled how she brought Sandra and me together; Max Bygraves told the story of the picture of a meal that he'd sent me; Josephine came down from Cheshire to talk of our school-days; Mike Medina and Brian Healy teased me about the Drumbeats and of course pride of place went to Sandra and the girls who were all looking absolutely beautiful for the occasion. I could see that the money for the party frocks was money well spent.

It was an incredible evening. Lovely, but completely

overwhelming. I enjoyed it, but I must say I'm glad it's all over and done with now and I can relax in the knowledge that no one goes on *This is your Life* twice.

After the show there was a big party. *This is your Life* parties are famous throughout Thames Television and I believe that mine was pretty good even by their standards. Unfortunately I don't remember much about it. By the time Sandra and I got back to the hotel I think I was pretty 'tired and emotional'.

CHAPTER 13

Moving On

In 1981 I left the BBC and moved on to Thames Television. For some reason there was an enormous fuss about it: the press declared I was going for more money, which was true, but that wasn't the most important reason.

Light entertainment is a priority at Thames, and they were able to make more money available for the production of my show. This meant that I could work a much slower pace than I'd previously been able to do.

At the BBC money was so tight that I often had to do as many as nine or ten characters a day in full make-up. I'd be in the studios by eight o'clock in the morning and didn't get away till ten at night. It was exhausting. At Thames I could do two or three characters in a day, take a day off and go back and do another three the day after. It was more relaxing and it eased the pressure on me.

It seemed sensible enough, and I couldn't understand why the press made so much of it. In fact, there were so many enquiries that Thames Television decided to hold a press conference. It was a bit embarrassing really: we sat at a table like heads of government and the managing director, Brian

Cowgill, presided over the meeting. The reporters asked questions like, 'How much are you being paid by Thames?'

'I don't know why you bother to ask,' I replied, 'because you know damn well I'm not going to tell you.'

'You might as well because if you don't we'll make it up,' said the reporter.

I refused to be drawn but the next day the *Daily Mirror* announced that I was moving to Thames for half a million pounds for a two-year contract. Of course it was nothing like that really, but I was flattered more than annoyed. It was nice to know that they thought people would be prepared to pay me that kind of money.

I wasn't without regrets at leaving the BBC. The day after the decision was announced, I bumped into Ian Trethowan, the Director General.

'We're very sorry to lose you, you know, Mike,' he said. I thought it was very kind of him to say so because it couldn't have made much difference to him.

'Well, I hope I haven't done my last show for the BBC,' I replied and I meant it.

Technically, in terms of lighting and sound, the BBC is far superior to the commercial stations and I felt homesick when I moved to Thames. Yet what I wanted more than anything was time. All my life I'd wanted to be a star. Now, when some people were describing me as a star, I sometimes felt like giving the whole thing up. I had the big house and the Rolls Royce but I was desperate for more time to enjoy them.

Throughout my career I'd resisted moving from my roots in the north of England. It made sense while northern clubland played such a big part in my career, but now most of the clubs were gone and I turned down more summer seasons than I accepted because I preferred to be at home. My work had become centred on Thames Television's studios in Teddington, Middlesex and suddenly it seemed crazy to live so far away. What was the point of spending £1,000 a week on hotel bills and half my life on the motorway, I thought? The logical solution was to move south.

Surprisingly Sandra, although a southerner herself, wasn't crazy about the idea because she'd made so many friends in Prestbury. Nevertheless she agreed it made sense. Our only worry was my mother.

Throughout the 1970s her illness had grown worse until it had reached the point where she scarcely put her nose outside the front door. Sometimes she'd look out of the window on lovely sunny days and say, 'I wish I could walk down to the bottom of the garden.'

There was nothing wrong with her legs. There was nothing physically wrong with her at all, but she believed the short walk out of doors was impossible for her and there was nothing you could say or do to make her change her mind.

The doctor came to see her and a psychiatrist called at the house, but nothing seemed to help. It got to the point where she even had a phobia about doctors and medical attention.

'I can help you. I might even be able to cure you,' the doctor pleaded, but she was afraid of the cure. She was afraid of almost everything.

During one of her better spells we managed to move her out of the cold, old fashioned little house in Bredbury to a new flat close to our home in Prestbury. It was a Regency style flat, very modern inside and well heated and it meant that Sandra and I could drop in frequently. My mother loved it – she'd always loved modern things. Yet her condition continued to deteriorate.

Gradually she developed anorexia nervosa on top of her other problems. She was so particular about her food and cared so deeply about the quality of it that we couldn't understand at first why she was growing so thin.

She had her favourite brands of just about every food you

could think of and she was convinced they were far superior to any others on the market. Nothing else would do. She minced best steak to make shepherd's pie, she drank one particular brand of tea and no other, and she would only buy cakes made at the bakers. Packet cakes went straight into the dustbin.

Josephine's son Tim still laughs about the time he visited his grandmother at teatime, taking with him a box of factory-made tarts. My mother threw them away and sent him back to the bakers to buy some 'proper' cakes.

Tim craftily bought another box of factory-made ones, removed them from their wrappers and put them in a paper bag. My mother found them very nice indeed and much better than that boxed rubbish Tim had brought earlier.

That was my mother. She liked the best and she took a great interest in food. Yet she wasn't eating it.

It was obvious that my mother wouldn't want to move south at her time of life. Even the thought of the journey was too much for her. Yet we didn't want to leave her and Dad stranded in Prestbury when we'd gone. Instead we bought them a house close to Josephine's in Marple Bridge, not far from the spot where they'd first met all those years ago.

My mother wasn't at all happy about us moving, but she realised it was the only sensible solution.

Sandra and I spent a lot of time house-hunting. Most of the houses were too expensive or not to our taste, but at last towards the end of 1982 an estate agent showed us a beautiful place in Walton-on-Thames. It had only just come on the market and the details hadn't yet been printed, which was just as well because it was the sort of place that was bound to be snapped up immediately.

It was a Tudor-style house with leaded windows, oak beams and oak panelling. There were five bedrooms upstairs, several very large rooms downstairs and there was a swimming pool, a tennis court and a sizeable landscaped garden.

We loved it. It cost more than we'd intended spending but from the moment we saw it we had to have it – it was like Old Dunbar all over again. We'll buy the house and worry about affording it afterwards, I thought.

We moved in in January 1983 and for weeks afterwards we were on a high, so thrilled to be living in this lovely house. Yet a couple of months later I felt a dreadful premonition that we weren't going to stay there. I'd left Cheshire, I'd left the BBC, now somehow I felt that everything was going to go wrong.

I tried to ignore the feeling and launched into another bout of extravagance. I had the tennis court resurfaced, I had the beams reconditioned, I changed an almost new and very expensive pale green carpet because beautiful as it was I didn't think it went well enough with our furniture. I even bought a grand piano costing £3,000.

'That's a good idea since you play so well,' said Sandra, knowing of course that I couldn't play a note.

'But Clare's learning,' I protested, 'and it'll come in useful when I'm rehearsing at home.'

That wasn't the reason of course. Clare soon gave up her lessons and there was no need for me to rehearse at home. I simply wanted a grand piano. I thought they looked nice.

I might even have had the swimming pool undersealed, but fortunately that was a Jimmy Tarbuck joke.

Jimmy's a great practical joker. I remember one night in the days before I was well known I called in to see him at a night club where he was appearing.

'Is it possible to go backstage and say hello to Jimmy?' I asked the compere.

'Yes, that'll be OK,' he said. 'Who shall I say it is?'

'Tell him it's Mike Yarwood.'

A few minutes later the compere reappeared and told me to come through. He led me through the back, behind the stage to the dressing room. The door was open and there was Jimmy grinning broadly.

'Now don't tell me, I'm good on names.'

'Come on, Jimmy, it's ...'

'No, don't tell me. I'll get it in a minute.'

We knew each other so well yet even I was beginning to wonder.

'Jimmy, don't be ridiculous, you know it's ...'

'Don't tell me!' He stared intently at me then shook his head, 'No, it's no good, I can't place you.'

'Jimmy it's me, Mike Yarwood.'

'Mike Yarwood? Mike Yarwood? Doesn't mean a thing.'

The compere was on the point of throwing me out when Jimmy suddenly roared with laughter.

'If you do Steptoe and Son I might recognise you!'

So not long after we moved into our house I shouldn't have been surprised when I got a call from the 'Water Board'.

'Mr Yarwood,' said an unfamiliar voice, 'I'm sorry to have to tell you that your swimming pool's leaking.'

'Leaking?' I said, alarmed. 'How can you tell?'

'At the Water Board we know these things.'

Now I know nothing about swimming pools but it seemed to me that a leak was serious and probably expensive.

'Can you do something about it?'

'I'm afraid, Mr Yarwood, that it's going to need underFsealing.'

'Undersealing? How much will that cost?'

'Well it's difficult to say over the phone. We'd need to inspect it. Will you be swimming in it today?'

It was only then that my suspicions were roused. It was a cold winter's day, and no ordinary person in their right mind would swim in an outdoor pool in that weather.

'Look, who am I speaking to?'

'Tarbuck's the name,' said the 'official', and Jimmy collapsed into laughter.

My own laughter was tinged with relief. I'd really bought the whole thing. Thank goodness the pool didn't need undersealing!

Socially we began to see a lot more of Jimmy and his wife now that we lived so much closer, and I walked into his traps nearly every time. One evening we were all going out together and Jimmy came to collect us.

'What car are you driving these days, Mike?' asked Jimmy as Sandra and I put on our coats.

'A BMW,' I said.

'A BMW? A BMW! I think that's disgusting.'

Jimmy sounded really annoyed and since I've always felt guilty about driving foreign cars it caught me on the raw.

'No, seriously, Mike, I'm not joking. That sort of thing makes me sick. A man in your position driving a foreign car. It's disgusting.'

He lectured me all the way outside, across the drive and out on to the pavement, where a large Mercedes was parked at the kerb. Jimmy Tarbuck, the man who hated people to drive foreign cars, owned a Mercedes! It was another of his jokes.

'You know it's funny you should pick on my BMW,' I told him as we drove away, 'because I've always felt bad about it. You really got me going.'

It's a good thing he wasn't serious. He might have persuaded me to buy another car.

I needed no encouragement to spend money. I spent money I didn't know I didn't have. I wasn't at all aware of financial things. When we'd lived at Old Dunbar I got away with my extravagance but now it caught up with me. I'd overreached myself and I was under pressure. The only solution was to do things I didn't want to do because I needed the money.

In the middle of this unhappy situation my mother's

condition deteriorated badly. For some time I'd known that she was going through hell. She wasn't suffering physical pain like someone with cancer, but she was suffering badly all the same. She seemed to have the effects of a hangover, the thick head, the dry mouth, the thumping heart, without having touched a drop of alcohol. She hated to talk about it and as the years went on and the news from the doctors got worse and worse she refused to discuss it at all.

During the summer of 1984 I was signed up for a summer season in Bournemouth. At forty years old after nearly twenty-five years in the business, at a time when I'd thought I would be able to put my feet up a bit, I was back on the road again.

I was very worried about my mother. The last time I'd seen her I was shocked by her appearance – she was little more than a skeleton. Brooding about it in my Bournemouth hotel, I decided to give her a ring.

At first I was relieved. She sounded pleased to hear my voice and she seemed to be in a cheerful mood. But as the conversation went on I realised there was something wrong – she was rambling. My mother had never rambled yet now she couldn't seem to keep the thread of the conversation. I was more disturbed than ever.

Ten days later my father telephoned to say that Mum had been taken into hospital. I was pleased – I thought they'd feed her up and make her better.

Sadly it was too late.

The next day was my day off so I flew up to Manchester to visit her. I didn't realise how serious her condition was until I walked into the ward and saw her lying asleep. She was so still and lifeless and her face was so drawn I thought she was dead. I was horrified. It wasn't my mother lying there. I knew then that she was dying.

I never spoke to her again. She didn't wake.

Walking down the corridor later as I was leaving I was

conscious of nurses and orderlies staring and nudging each other and all but asking for autographs as if nothing was happening. Surely they must know, I thought; why can't they leave me alone?

My mother died the next day. She was sixty-seven.

It was an awful time. I felt terribly alone, as if a second umbilical cord had been cut. Part of me had gone. Josephine told me that she had seen Mum after she died and that she looked lovely. All the suffering had left her face and she was beautiful again. I can imagine what she meant and I wished I'd seen her too. It's not morbid: I would have liked to have seen her like that instead of the way she was when she was dying. I was pretty cut up about it for weeks, then I started to feel relieved that her suffering was over. She's better off now, I told myself. I couldn't wish her back to all that.

After my mother's death the financial pressures increased. I worked harder than ever and grew more depressed. I was painfully aware of the penalties comics seemed to pay for overworking. Eric Morecambe, Dick Emery and Tommy Cooper had all died suddenly and one night I thought it was going to happen to me.

Everyone suffers from stage fright but I'd never felt that I couldn't go on stage until I went to Felixstowe. There a bad dream came true.

I'd done the first show without any problems and between performances I went for a meal with some friends. I felt perfectly normal. I returned to the theatre, put on my make-up and got as far as the wings when awful pins and needles pains shot up my left arm. They got worse and worse, and I was sure I was having a heart attack. Theatrical people tend to think it always takes you whilst you're on the stage, and I couldn't go through with it. I just couldn't go on. Some part of me was saying you can't handle this any more, and I started to believe it. They were playing my music and I couldn't move.

It's the sort of thing you see in the movies, the sort of thing you dream about, but this was actually happening.

The manager came running up.

'What's the matter? They're playing your music.'

'I'm ill,' I gasped.

The recent deaths were in everyone's minds so the show was cancelled and I was rushed to hospital. Fortunately there was nothing wrong. They gave me a thorough check-up and said I must have been suffering from stage fright.

This diagnosis was almost as worrying as if they'd told me there was something wrong with my heart. Surely I'm not going to have to go through that again, I thought. If it happens again I'm finished.

Waiting for my next show was hell. I wouldn't know whether or not I could go on until the very last minute. I've got to go through with it, I told myself. As it happened the next show was fine, and I've been perfectly all right ever since. I expect it was a combination of tension and tiredness from overwork, but it was a frightening experience.

My premonition seemed to be coming true. Everything was indeed going wrong and there was worse to come. In December our marriage broke up.

It was all my fault. The heavy drinking, the separations and my hang-ups about going out had all taken their toll on our relationship. I had been selfish and inconsiderate. Looking back I realised I'd planned my whole life around myself. I didn't plan it for us, I planned it for me – what I wanted to do, where I wanted to go, even down to what I wanted to watch on television. Sandra is unselfish to the point where people walk all over her and I took advantage of it. Sometimes I realised what was happening and tried to be unselfish too, but she was very difficult to compete with.

'It's not a competition,' Sandra used to say.

'But I've got to live with you and be good enough for you,'

I said. But it was very hard for me and I soon slipped back into my old ways.

I suppose the break-up was inevitable. Twice before Sandra had wanted to split up and I had managed to talk her out of it, but this time I didn't even try. If it was going to happen anyway, there seemed to be no point in prolonging the agony. We might as well get it over with.

A few days after we'd decided on a trial separation (though we were still living in the same house), the press found out. How it leaked I'll never know, but one day when Sandra was out a reporter from the *Daily Mirror* came to the door. There was no point in asking how he'd heard because he wouldn't have told me anyway. What's more, I knew it would get out sooner or later so I thought I would stick my fingers down my throat and get it over with. I know it sounds crude, but that's how I felt.

I invited him in and when I finished talking to him, I spoke to all the other newspapers. Right, that's it, I thought, that's the end of it.

I was wrong. The next morning we were amazed to discover that we were front page news. There were no big stories about at the time, but even so I couldn't believe people would be that interested.

Sandra hated it, and it was a horrible feeling having your dirty linen washed in public like that. It didn't even stop there. We refused to do any more interviews so the journalists came and camped on our doorstep. Sandra opened the door a couple of times and told them politely that we had nothing to add. I ignored them, but on one occasion when she was out a reporter kept knocking on the door and when I refused to answer it he shouted questions through the letterbox.

It went on and on. Sandra was particularly annoyed when the *Daily Express*, having been denied an interview, promptly rehashed some six-year old quotes and brought them up to date by adding, 'said Sandra last night,' as if the conversation had just taken place.

Even when the initial fuss died down, some papers hung on. There was a little red car parked just up the road for days. I knew who it belonged to and I knew which paper they were from. They sat out there watching the comings and goings from the house and even tried to follow me one day. It was quite fun in a way. I'll give them the slip, I thought, just like in the movies. Since I had a much faster car it wasn't difficult to lose them and I got quite a kick out of that.

I suppose they didn't believe there was no one else involved and they wanted to catch one of us out with a mystery girlfriend or boyfriend, but of course there was nothing like that.

It was May before we sold our beautiful house. The months in between when we were living together yet not living together were very sad. It was particularly painful to think that it had happened in the lovely house that had given us so much pleasure when we first moved in. Now it would belong to someone else.

For the first time in sixteen years of marriage Sandra and I went house-hunting separately. Eventually our joint home was sold and Sandra and the girls moved to Weybridge and I to Cobham.

I hadn't taken much interest in the house in Cobham. I didn't really want to move from Walton-on-Thames so I didn't bother much about the place I moved into. I wanted something convenient, that was all.

Yet inadvertently I chose another family house. It was new and close to the motorway but far too large for one man living on his own.

The split was as amicable as possible for the children's sake. You might divorce your husband or wife but you can't divorce your children. And in fact we didn't even discuss divorce.

There's no need since neither of us wants to marry again at the moment.

I was making a television show while all this upheaval was going on and I'm afraid I let it slip a bit. I went through a period when I thought to hell with it, how dare this happen to me? How *could* this happen to me? My marriage had broken up; why the hell should I knock myself out now?

It took me quite a while to realise I was only punishing myself.

CHAPTER 14

At the Crossroads

The supermarket was bewildering. All around me were shelves of food but I didn't know what to do. I picked up a couple of tins and carried them towards the counter. This was going to take all day if you had a lot of shopping, I thought.

'Where are you going, Daddy?' asked Clare. 'There are baskets for your shopping.'

I looked round. I hadn't noticed the stack of baskets beside the door. I went back, picked one up and started to fill it. At the fruit counter I piled apples on top of my other purchases.

'Excuse me,' said the fruit assistant, 'there are bags for the fruit.' She pointed to a roll of polythene bags nearby.

'Oh yes,' I said, tearing one off. Embarrassed, I transferred the apples to the polythene bag and was about to drop it back into the basket when Clare stopped me.

'Daddy, you have to get them *weighed* first,' she whispered.

Supermarket shopping was obviously more complicated than I thought. During my marriage I had been so spoiled that I'd never been into a supermarket before and I didn't know what to do. I do now of course. One more rehearsal and I'll really have it off pat!

When I lived at home with my parents my mother looked after me so well that when I got married at the age of twenty-eight I couldn't take the top off my boiled egg. Sandra taught me how to get into my egg but in most other respects she took over from my mother. She did everything for me – she ran the house, looked after the secretarial work, the household accounts and my financial affairs. When I went away she packed my cases for me and if I had to catch a plane she took me to the airport, checked in my luggage, sorted out my ticket and generally got me organised.

I was completely helpless yet I encouraged her. I had the attitude, 'I'm the star, don't bother me with trivial details'. I thought I shouldn't have to worry about anything except my performance.

The break-up of my marriage changed all that. I think it's going to be good for me. I'm forced to do things for myself now. I can't rely on other people and I will probably become more confident as a result. Already I've discovered that it's not as difficult to look after a house as I thought.

For a time I was pretty unhappy. I started getting depressed and whenever I get depressed I start to think that the bubble has burst and my career's on the way down. An appearance on the *Bob Hope 82nd Birthday Show* didn't help.

When I was first asked if I would like to take part I was really excited because I've been an admirer of Bob Hope's for years. What's more, the show was to be screened in America and I've always wanted to get into the American market.

'We'd like you to do two spots,' they said, 'one as Bob Hope in full make-up, the works.'

'Terrific,' I said, 'but isn't he on the show?'

'No, he's sitting in the Royal Box with Prince Philip. He's the guest of honour. The other impression we would like you to do is Prince Charles.'

'Fine,' I said.

I hadn't felt so nervous since I was a beginner in the business. Travelling to the theatre where the show was to be performed I felt the old chill down my spine and the hair on the back of my neck started to lift.

The first hint of problems came soon after I arrived. Bob Hope would be appearing in the show after all, it seemed. One of my rules is that I don't do impressions of people on the same show, but it was too late to change things now. Apprehensively I sat down to watch Bob's rehearsal, and my worst fears were realised – Bob and I were covering the same topics.

When he'd finished I went over. We were introduced then I said, 'I've just watched your routine and I noticed you've got a lot of Reagan material, a thing about Thatcher and one about Gerry Ford. I'm doing exactly the same people, though with different gags of course ...'

'Well that's OK,' said Bob pleasantly, 'only I wouldn't do anything about Reagan. It wouldn't do for both of us.'

'What about Thatcher?'

'Well I wouldn't ...'

At this point the producer, sensing trouble, interrupted.

'We'll sort it out, don't worry,' he told me. He took Bob aside and obviously said, 'If you start taking all this stuff out he's going to have a big hole in his act and he'll get despondent.'

A little later Bob came back and asked for just two changes. He wanted me to drop the Gerry Ford gag and also a reference to Concorde because he was doing one on Pan Am. I was happy to oblige.

I started my rehearsal and immediately ran into more problems. My first appearance was to be in full Bob Hope costume and make-up. The audience wouldn't have seen Mike Yarwood beforehand, so I wanted an announcement to be made: 'By arrangement with Mike Yarwood – Bob Hope.'

The producer shook his head. 'No, no. We'll just announce Bob Hope.'

I tried to explain that this wasn't a good idea. The audience would know that Bob Hope was on the show and for a few moments there would be confusion – they'd think I really was Bob Hope. The producer didn't think this was a problem.

Unhappily I carried on until we came to the Prince Charles slot.

'And now we have Prince Charles ...' said the announcer.

'You can't announce him like that,' I said to the producer. 'Prince Charles would never be announced in that way. They'd say "His Royal Highness The Prince of Wales".'

'Prince of Wales? Nobody knows anything about the Prince of Wales in America,' said the producer. 'It's got to be Prince Charles.'

And so it went on. He probably put me down as a troublemaker.

Yet despite these irritations the show went well, my act was practically intact and Bob Hope himself was very nice. I was pleased with the whole thing. It was only later that I discovered what had happened.

In America where the show was edited my act was drastically cut. Just about every gag that got a round of applause was removed, and the Reagan references virtually disappeared. Lines like, 'All these rumours about Reagan's hair not being natural ... his hair is quite natural. It's the colour hair goes after grey ...' which got a good laugh at the time were cut out, leaving me with a limp, unamusing act. The Prince Charles slot was removed altogether.

So America's first taste of Mike Yarwood was an unfunny impression of Bob Hope. Worse still, Thames Television bought the programme after it had been cut and therefore couldn't restore the best pieces of my act. They had to screen it as it was, so no doubt the British public thought I was slipping too.

I was bitterly disappointed. It might sound bitchy but I'm

convinced it happened because my script was better than Bob's. I'd used some of Bob's own writers to make my impression more authentic and they'd excelled themselves that day, though you would never have guessed it from what appeared on screen.

I can only hope that if I ever become a big international star like Bob Hope and I'm still in the business at the age of eighty-two I could be different.

The incident did nothing to ease my depression. Instead I moved house again to a smaller place that felt more comfortable, I started preparation for my next show, and I had Charlotte and Clare to stay for two weeks. Having the kids changed things completely. Suddenly all was not lost.

Before they arrived I found myself regretting more than ever that I hadn't spent enough time with them when they were small. I remember little things like the time when Clare, then a toddler, wouldn't settle one night so in the end I brought her downstairs and sat her next to me on the sofa while I watched television. The television would soon send her to sleep, I reasoned.

Instead she was riveted, and when the programme finished she said, 'Are there any more children's programmes on, Daddy?' And I'd been watching *The Sweeney*!

Then there was the time Charlotte asked if I could borrow Sandra's small car when I collected her from school because she was embarrassed when I came in the Rolls. I've often been tactless with Charlotte over the years. She's keen to go into show business and one day she got an audition for a part in a television programme.

'When she comes downstairs say something encouraging,' Sandra warned me. 'No matter what you think say something encouraging.'

'Of course I'll say something encouraging,' I said, pouring another cup of tea. 'What do you take me for?'

A few moments later Charlotte walked in and the first thing I saw was masses of make-up plastered all over her pretty face.

'You've got too much make-up on; you'll blow it,' I said before I could stop myself.

'Oh wonderful. Very encouraging,' said Sandra.

I could have kicked myself. I knew I was right and in fact Charlotte didn't get the part, but I could have said it in a more tactful way.

Despite all this Charlotte seems to have forgiven me and we had an enjoyable fortnight when they came to stay. Clare is horse-mad and she goes to the stables straight after school, so Charlotte and I did the cooking. It wasn't anything elaborate, mainly oven-ready food and omelettes, but it was nice working together in the kitchen preparing the meal.

I spoiled them by letting them have white bread too, instead of the wholemeal Sandra prefers them to eat. I wasn't trying to score points over Sandra; I just thought it wouldn't hurt to give them a little treat now and again.

The girls constantly amaze us. Physically I don't think they resemble either Sandra or me – I can't think who they take after. In personality Clare is very like Sandra: she has the same placid nature and dislike of inactivity. Charlotte is more like me. She's a very good mimic, she wants to go into show business and she has a tremendous ability to loaf. If I'm not careful I could happily loaf all day and get nothing done, and unfortunately for her, Charlotte's just the same.

Our fortnight together seemed to speed by. We didn't do anything special: I acted as chauffeur most of the time – collecting the girls from school, running backwards and forwards to the stables or the homes of various friends. In the evenings we watched television together. It was quiet but nice, and when they'd gone the house seemed very empty without them.

These days I'm getting used to living alone, though it was

strange at first after all those years of marriage. I don't mean to sound self-pitying. I'm not always alone after all – sometimes there's someone with me – but the problem is that I don't want to get involved in another serious relationship and the sort of women I like are the sort who deserve more than a one-night stand. Consequently I'm on my own quite a lot. Yet it's not as bad for me as it must be for other men who find themselves in the same position, because I've spent so much time alone in hotel rooms during my marriage that I've grown used to my own company.

There are pluses to the single life too. I enjoy being my own man. When I get up in the morning I don't have to worry about what sort of mood I'm in as there's no one to inflict myself upon. I also have that precious early morning time all to myself. I like to get up very early, about five-thirty in the morning during summer, make myself a pot of coffee and just be on my own for at least an hour and a half. I love that time of day when everything's waking up. Now I can enjoy it without fear of being disturbed.

Sometimes I think I could quite easily become a recluse if I'm not careful. I've definitely got reclusive tendencies: I like to shut myself away if I don't feel good and I wonder if I'll end up like Howard Hughes. Then again I'm sure I won't because I recognise the danger and guard against it.

In some ways the separation has even improved my relationship with Sandra. I still see her every week and the four of us have a regular date for Sunday lunch. These days she's more honest with me. She told me not long ago that she didn't like my last show. She told me what was wrong with it and the reason – that I hadn't worked hard enough. At the time my ego was severely dented but afterwards I realised she was quite right. When we were living together Sandra would never have said that. She was always the sort of person who hated to offend anyone, least of all me. Now she's more honest and it's good for me.

But if Sandra has become a tougher critic, she still can't compete with my daughters. They've always been my most difficult audience. I like to make people laugh all the time, not just when I'm getting paid for it. If I've said something funny in the office at Teddington and everybody has laughed, I look back when I come home and I think I did well today, I got a big laugh. Yet it's very difficult to make the girls laugh. As small children they liked my Frank Spencer and Ken Dodd impressions but they preferred the real characters. Now they seem to laugh most when I'm not even trying to be funny. For example, first thing in the morning when I get up my hair is sticking out in about twenty different directions because I'm a restless sleeper, and they find that hilarious.

Looking back over my life it's difficult to believe that it's twenty-five years since I first got up in front of an unknown audience and went through my impressions. I'm amazed I'm still doing it. When I started out impressionists were more or less speciality acts and they usually went on to other things. Peter Sellers, Max Bygraves and many others began as impressionists and moved on. Now being a mimic is a career in itself and there seems to be an epidemic of them.

People often ask whether it makes me edgy to see a good impressionist on television, and I reply that it only makes me edgy if I see a bad one. A good impressionist gives me a lot of pleasure, and someone else being good is not going to make me any worse. I admire anyone who does it well.

These days I sometimes get kids writing to me to ask how to become a mimic. I write back and ask whether they can do impressions now. It's no use saying they want to learn to become a mimic – I think mimics are born, not made. You might be able to go to drama school and learn to act but you can't teach mimicry.

I'm sure that an inferiority complex made me a mimic. If I think of a funny line I'll say it as Eric Morecambe or John Cleese or Frankie Howerd. Lack of confidence makes me feel that it wouldn't be so funny if I said it as me.

Max Bygraves once summed it up. He said the strange thing about me is that I'm not a very good stand-up comic, yet when I *do* a stand-up comic, I'm great. It's the same with my singing. I'm an awful singer but when I do an impression of a singer my voice isn't bad.

I can't explain it. The ability to do it must be there inside me, but when I'm Mike Yarwood it doesn't come out.

Now I think of impressionism almost as an art form in its own right. I would hate to be misunderstood as the fella who takes the mickey out of people. I never intend to be unkind. What I'm trying to do is create a person. Just as mime artist Marcel Marceau can create wind or an invisible sheet of glass with his mime and make you believe it's there, so I want to make people believe that the character I'm mimicking is there. But that's all. It's not satire; I'm not putting across a point of view; I'm just creating a person as accurately as I know how.

I think it's cruel to draw attention to someone's physical imperfections. Sometimes the make-up girls have said to me, so and so's got bad teeth; would you like us to put that in, and I say no. I don't want to do anything that would embarrass the individual concerned or make him feel uncomfortable watching my act in front of his family. Families can be very sensitive.

Comedians sometimes make jokes about me these days.

'Mike Yarwood rang me up and said, "Could you give me some advice?"' said one comedian recently. '"Every time I sing I don't know what to do with my hands." Put them over your mouth I told him.'

I roared with laughter when I heard that because I thought

it was very funny, but the girls didn't like it at all. They get upset when people make jokes about me, particularly if they're unkind jokes.

I prefer to do impressions of real people when I can, and I think of fictional characters as cheating. I break my own rules quite often because of popular demand, but I don't really like doing the Basil Fawltys, the Alf Garnetts and the Frank Spencers, because they are characters invented by other people and belong to their creators.

I found Basil Fawlty exhausting because I never felt physically like him. Inspector Clouseau, Peter Sellers' brilliant invention, was almost as difficult. I'd forgotten that Sellers was a genius and I'm not.

So many comic actors are over the top. Peter Sellers was always *under* the top. He never over-sold a line, he just said it, and I've never seen him 'mug' (pull a face) in my life. When he fell backwards into a swimming pool or out of a window his face was almost blank – his eyes held the only expression. You could see that he knew he was going but he was hoping no one would notice. It looks so simple, but in fact it's about the most difficult thing you can do.

When it was suggested that I do Clouseau on my show, Big Mouth me had to say at rehearsals, 'We must do one of those falls he does backwards. They're marvellous. I desperately want to do one of those falls.'

What I'd forgotten was that I don't like heights and to fall seven or eight feet out of a window, backwards, even when there was a pile of mattresses and two stunt supervisors to catch me, was a frightening experience. I badly wanted to mug. In the end I managed to hold my face long enough but it was clear to me that I was a long way from being Peter Sellers.

I have a lot of idols in the business: Peter Sellers was one, and Laurence Olivier is another. Olivier is a brilliant mimic, a hundred times better than I am because the characters he creates and mimics are only written on a piece of paper.

The only time I ever get irritated with other impressionists is when I know they're merely copying me, that they haven't looked at the character but just at me doing the character.

What they've forgotten is that I improvise and invent things for the character to do, and I say things that the character hasn't actually said, but might have said. For example, Max Bygraves didn't say, 'I wanna tell you a story ...' Hughie Green didn't say, 'And I mean that most sincerely, friends.' I invented those catchphrases so when I hear another impressionist using them I know he's studied me and not the subject.

Mind you, sometimes the subject ends up using the catchphrase himself. When I was doing Danny La Rue I put in the catchphrase, 'Isn't that right, Jack?'

Danny did actually say this but not on stage. Jack used to be his manager and during conversations Danny was always turning to Jack for confirmation and saying, 'Isn't that right, Jack?'

Not long ago Danny told me he's now forced to use the phrase in his act.

'People expect me to include it because they think that's what I really do say,' he complained.

'Well, you do,' I pointed out.

'Yes, but never on stage.'

He does now. I suppose that's the ultimate compliment.

These days I feel very much at the crossroads. After twenty-five years in the business I would like to branch out and try something new, but I'm unsure which direction to take. I know I'll never stop being a mimic – I can't help but mimic what I see – but I'd like to do something else as well.

For twenty-five years I've had a love-hate relationship with show business. If I hadn't been in the business I might still be happily married, I might not have started drinking heavily, my childhood shyness might not have returned, I might not feel self-conscious in public places and I might not suffer bursts of anxiety and depression. Alternatively, if I hadn't been in the business I probably wouldn't have driven a Rolls-Royce, I wouldn't have had a house with a swimming pool and tennis court, I wouldn't have been invited to parties at 10 Downing Street or met members of the royal family, and my name wouldn't appear in *Who's Who*. And if I hadn't been in show business I wouldn't have written this book.

Fontana Paperbacks:
Non-fiction

Fontana is a leading paperback publisher of non-fiction, both popular and academic.

- ☐ The Relaxation Response *Herbert Benson* £1.75
- ☐ Once a Month *Katharina Dalton* £2.95
- ☐ The Cinderella Complex *Colette Dowling* £2.95
- ☐ Jealousy *Nancy Friday* £3.95
- ☐ My Mother My Self *Nancy Friday* £2.95
- ☐ A Woman's Guide to Alternative Medicine *Liz Grist* £3.95
- ☐ Victims of Violence *Joan Jonker* £2.95
- ☐ Talking to a Stranger *Lindsay Knight* £2.95
- ☐ Relief Without Drugs *Ainslie Meares* £1.95
- ☐ Miscarriage *Ann Oakley, Ann McPherson & Helen Roberts* £2.50
- ☐ Controlling Chronic Pain *Connie Peck* £2.95
- ☐ Living with Loss *Liz McNeil Taylor* £1.75
- ☐ Postnatal Depression *Vivienne Welburn* £2.50
- ☐ The Courage to Change *Dennis Wholey* £2.95

You can buy Fontana paperbacks at your local bookshop or newsagent. Or you can order them from Fontana Paperbacks, Cash Sales Department, Box 29, Douglas, Isle of Man. Please send a cheque, postal or money order (not currency) worth the purchase price plus 22p per book for postage (maximum postage required is £3).

NAME (Block letters) _____

ADDRESS _____

_____

_____

While every effort is made to keep prices low, it is sometimes necessary to increase them at short notice. Fontana Paperbacks reserve the right to show new retail prices on covers which may differ from those previously advertised in the text or elsewhere.